W9-AZV-819

2 to 22 DAYS IN THAILAND

THE ITINERARY PLANNER

DERK RICHARDSON

John Muir Publications
Santa Fe, New Mexico

John Muir Publications, P.O. Box 613, Santa Fe, NM 87504

First printing. August 1993

ISSN 1062-4570
ISBN 1-56261-118-6

Distributed to the book trade by:
W. W. Norton & Company, Inc.
New York, New York

Design Mary Shapiro
Maps Janice St. Marie
Typography Richard Harris
Printer Banta Company
Cover photo Leo de Wys Inc./Steve Vidler

CONTENTS

CONTENTS

ACKNOWLEDGMENTS

Research for this book was made immeasurably easier and more enjoyable by the company of my wife, Robin, who shared the difficulties of the work and the joys of discovery. The values and visions we hold in common have been reaffirmed in our travels together. We dedicate this edition to our special friends in Chiang Mai (Pitaya and Dang) and Chiang Rai (Jane, June, Too and Uan). Burl Willes, Roger Rapoport, and Peter Beren set the wheels in motion and helped keep them rolling along the way. Diane Clark Johnson graciously supplied Thai contacts from her extensive culinary travels. In Bangkok, Mr. Chaisong Churitt, Ms. Pataraporn (Lek) Sithivanich, and Mr. Satit Nillwongse of the Tourism Authority of Thailand provided invaluable assistance. Throughout Thailand, on every stop along the way, new friends and acquaintances, too many to cite individually, contributed their knowledge and hospitality toward the completion of this project. At John Muir Publications, I thank the entire staff for seeing the manuscript through to its final form.

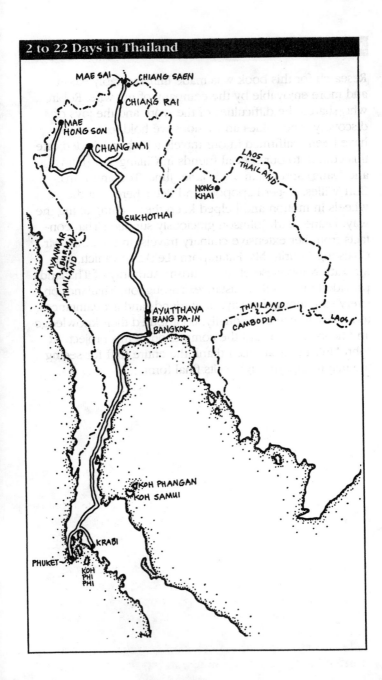

HOW TO USE THIS BOOK

There will never be a better time for a 22-day vacation in Thailand. One of the fastest-developing countries in Southeast Asia, Thailand is attracting greater numbers of tourists every year, but it is not yet overrun. From the teeming and exciting megalopolis of Bangkok to remote hill tribe villages in the north and deserted white sand beaches in the south, Thailand offers a uniquely diverse and exotic array of pleasures for the adventurous traveler. And it is all still available at a bargain.

During the past four years, I have taken several trips to Southeast Asia, searching out the kinds of sights, accommodations, and restaurants I would recommend to my friends. Previous projects for John Muir Publications have included researching and contributing to major portions of Burl Willes's *Undiscovered Islands of the Caribbean* and contributing the chapters on Thailand and Bali to Burl Willes's and Roger Rapoport's *2 to 22 Days in Asia* and *22 Days Around the World*. The lessons learned in those explorations have been refined for *2 to 22 Days in Thailand*.

The year 1987 was officially designated "Visit Thailand Year" by the Thai government, and in response to aggressive advertising and conscientious development of the tourist industry, the number of tourists jumped more than 23 percent to a record 3.5 million. It rose another 750,000 in 1988. Tourism was up more than 10 percent in 1990, but has dipped considerably since the Gulf War. The average stay has been about a week, indicating that most visitors missed many of Thailand's less promoted attractions. Tourism from the United States is gradually increasing but still remains a tiny portion of the overall profile, about 5 percent. But Americans are heartily welcomed in Thailand, and a surprising number of Thais speak English.

In planning and testing this 22-day itinerary, I have designed a trip that I would like to repeat, either as an

independent traveler or as a member of a group who
would be likely to break away from a tight schedule and
get off the beaten track. Although recommendations are
made for indulgent splurges, the itinerary is aimed largely
at the traveler who might chafe in a deluxe package yet
wants a few more amenities than a backpack and a
sleeping bag. It is flexible enough, however, to be used
as a complement to either a luxury plan or a by-the-seat-
of-the-pants roughing-it trip.

The book concentrates on three regions: Bangkok and
its environs; the northern hill country around Chiang Mai,
Chiang Rai, and Mae Hong Son; and the southern islands.
It covers a lot of territory, but the itinerary is manageable,
allowing you time to experience each area fully without
rushing around frantically to see it all. By not trying to be
exhaustive, it won't leave you exhausted at the end of
what is, after all, a vacation. It is not an encyclopedic
"been there, seen that" guide but rather aims to give you
a wide variety of rich and rewarding experiences. To that
end, the book is divided into daily itinerary sections,
each containing:

1. A **general overview** of each day.

2. **Suggested schedules** for travel, sightseeing, shopping, and meals.

3. Summaries of major **sightseeing highlights** (rated
▲▲▲ Don't miss; ▲▲ Try hard to see; ▲ Worthwhile if
you can make it), with step-by-step walking tours and
excursion directions to the most important sights.

4. **Food and accommodations suggestions**, from bargain and moderately priced favorites to deluxe splurges.

5. **Helpful hints**—random tidbits that will help make
your trip go well.

6. **Itinerary options**—excursion suggestions for travelers who have more time.

7. **Maps** designed to show you walking routes and
how to find recommended restaurants and sightseeing
highlights.

Why Thailand?

The subject of numerous stereotypes and clichés, from Yul Brynner's preening monarch in *The King and I* to the travel poster hype of "The Land of Smiles," Thailand cannot be summed up in any single image. And that is the key to its appeal. From the hills and jungles of the Golden Triangle through the dense urban metropolis of Bangkok to the white sand beaches and turquoise waters of its southern peninsula, Thailand is one of the most diverse and complex countries in Asia. It is a many-faceted society held together in an intricate web of culture, religion, and political independence. It is a region of countless contradictions and delicious complexities, fascinating history and intriguing contemporary development, all of which are more easily and economically accessible to the inquisitive traveler than in most other Asian countries. The culture is a mix of ancient ways and modern customs, and the society balances precariously between a wild urban sprawl and an abiding sense of rural peace and harmony. Material wealth is being amassed through industry and entrepreneurial endeavor in the shadow of widespread poverty. Social and economic gaps are widening, while certain fundamental, unifying beliefs and values have not yet lost their hold on the population.

If you are looking for a destination with myriad possibilities, Thailand is unsurpassed. It includes one of the great cities of Asia, Bangkok, with centuries of history captured in spectacular temples and ornate palaces alongside skyscrapers reaching for the future; it is a Buddhist culture in the trappings of modern society; it provides the chance to trek among primitive hill tribes living according to ancient tradition in the northern mountains; and it fits any expectation of what a tropical paradise should be with its palm-studded islands in the Andaman Sea and the Gulf of Thailand. Accommodations range from primitive one-room beach bungalows to luxury hotels and everything in between.

The geography is a unique panorama of dense jungles, untamed rivers, mountainous retreats, vast plains of rice paddies, brilliant white sand beaches, and warm, clear ocean waters. Occupying the central and western part of the Indochinese Peninsula, with Myanmar (formerly Burma) to the west, Laos to the north, Kampuchea to the east, and Malaysia to the south, Thailand covers 513,115 square kilometers (20,525 sq. mi.), about the size of France, or California and New York State combined. Its mountainous north, geologically linked to the great Himalayan range, slopes down into a semiarid northeastern plateau and fertile central plain. The country squeezes into a narrow isthmus in the south, bordered by the Gulf of Thailand and the Andaman Sea. Thailand's tropical climate supports myriad forms of vegetation— including over 1,000 varieties of orchids—and animal life; elephants, tigers, snakes, birds, and monkeys.

It is difficult to find such variety, in such an inviting tropical climate, anywhere else in the world. It is also hard to imagine such an array of bargains, including inexpensive accommodations, sumptuous meals for a few dollars, and low-priced handicrafts and antiques as well as designer copies. Nor are you likely to encounter another native people so consistently friendly, sharing meals, stories, customs, and helpful information, always with a genuine smile. Thailand's ethnically mixed population of 60 million descends mostly from Mon, Khmer, and Thai peoples but has absorbed waves of migration from China as well. Ninety-five percent of the people are Buddhist. Islam is the largest minority religion, with about 2 million adherents, and about 200,000 Thais are Christians. Men typically spend three months in the monkhood as they become adults. The abiding spirituality underpins the Thai people's universally kind and friendly demeanor.

And, of course, Thailand is home to one of the great cuisines of the world. Thai food is reaching unprecedented peaks of popularity in the West. Thai restaurants are cropping up in cities all over the United States and Europe. The characteristic spices, the savory blend of fresh ingredients, and the methods of preparation are influencing cooking styles from California to Paris. But nothing compares to sampling the real thing, in all its local variations, day after day, in its native land.

If you have never been to Thailand, this book will help you discover why so many first-time visitors plan second and third trips. If you are returning, it will guide you to new discoveries. The itinerary will direct you to many of the most significant attractions in Thailand; more important, it will provide intimate glimpses into unusual places, lesser-known sights, and special restaurants (many of which were tested—and relished—repeatedly). It is specific and detailed but also flexible; contract or expand it according to your personal interests. If you must take a shorter trip, focus on the most interesting highlights. If you have more time at your disposal, explore the options and extend your visits to the places that attract you.

Visiting Thailand is easier than ever before. Airfares will be the biggest portion of your expenditures, but trans-Pacific competition makes it possible to find surprising bargains. Asian languages are often seen as a barrier to travel, and the tonal Thai language is extremely difficult to master. Pronunciation is so complex and crucial that phrase books tend to be of little help. But tourism has become the country's major industry, giving rise to an efficient infrastructure of plane, train, bus, and taxi transportation. And most people involved with travelers speak some English and make great efforts to help you enjoy their country.

You should consider making your trip soon. Thailand, like all of Asia, is changing quickly. The emphasis on Western-style development and the concerted efforts to attract tourists from all over the world cannot help but create sharper economic, social, and cultural contrasts. While the country's economy is modernizing rapidly, exporting tin, rubber, and textiles, three-quarters of the population work in agriculture, mostly related to the enormous rice production. Much village life remains insulated from twentieth-century cultural customs, even while the modern market economy increases the burden of debt for rural farmers. Increased tourism does provide an incentive for historical and environmental preservation, but it can also propel a society toward commercialization and the exploitation of resources. How you spend your travel dollar weighs heavily in the balance. Thailand has much that is precious and deserving of special care, from the thousands of temples and the indigenous culture of the hill tribes to dwindling teak forests and the fragile coral reefs of the coastal waters.

Following this itinerary, you will start your trip through Thailand in Bangkok, venture north into the tribal hill country, then south to a series of secluded islands, and finally back to Bangkok before your departure. For each area, the book contains favorite temples, excursions, walks, hotels, guest houses, restaurants, shops, and beaches. In Bangkok, you will tour the Grand Palace and such stunning temples as Wat Pho and Wat Benchamabopit, cruise the river arteries, take a side trip to the ancient capital of Ayutthaya, and still have time for shopping and nightlife. Every meal will be a revelation.

Your next stop is Chiang Rai, near the famous Golden Triangle region at the borders of Thailand, Burma, and Laos. In addition to excursions into the hill country, you'll have dinner at one of Thailand's most creative (and largely undiscovered) restaurants and meet a fascinating artisan who specializes in fantastic hand-carved ladles. Chiang Mai, Thailand's second-largest city, is the north's hub of commerce and handicrafts and home to an exciting night bazaar full of exotic goods and surprising bargains. Mae Hong Son, to the west, is a small, friendly provincial town nestled in an idyllic setting of foggy mountains and winding rivers. You can explore the morning market with few other Westerners around, and you'll be able to plan your own trek into the jungle to meet and stay with hill tribe people.

The islands of southern Thailand are unsurpassed for their combination of scenic beauty, secluded beaches, fresh seafood, and friendly people. You'll start at Koh Samui, a developing resort island that still offers plenty of privacy, and have the option of discovering more remote neighboring islands. After a stop in the fascinating penin-sula province of Krabi, where you can explore caves, botanical gardens, and an ancient shell cemetery, you'll wind up your southern jaunt on Koh Phi Phi, the epito-me of tropical island paradise. After a day of snorkeling or scuba diving, you can enjoy fresh barbecued lobster or bonita while watching the sunset over Phi Phi Don's towering limestone cliffs. On your last day in Bangkok, you can get in some last-minute shopping for silks, cloth-ing, wood carvings, and souvenirs, take in another tem-ple, or savor a final meal in one of the city's world-class restaurants before heading home.

Getting There

More than a dozen international airlines have regular ser-vice into Bangkok, and the competition means tremen-dous bargains are available, especially in the low season. Thai Airways is renowned for its comfort, service, and in-flight cuisine, and round-trip fares on special occasions as low as $880 put the cost within reach of moderate budgets. Singapore Airlines, Garuda Indonesia, Canadian-Pacific, Northwest Orient, Malaysian Air, and others fly into Bangkok with wide-bodied DC10s and 747s for less than $1,000 round-trip.

Cathay Pacific and Garuda Indonesia also offer circle-Pacific fares, which include Hong Kong and Bali and start at $1,350 in the low season from the West Coast, $1,450 in the high season.

If you deal with a travel agent who does substantial business in Asia and works through a consolidator, or discount broker, you may be able to get an even better deal—as much as $250 off the full-price fare. You can find advertisements for discount fares in such newspa-

pers as the *Village Voice* and the *New York Times* in the
East and the *San Francisco Examiner-Chronicle* and the
Los Angeles Times in the West. Not all consolidators are
bonded, unlike accredited travel agents, so if you buy
directly from such a broker, you shouldn't pay until you
have your ticket in hand. You can find useful information
about consolidators and discount fares in the winter
1988-89 issue of the *Offbeat Tours* newsletter, available
for $5 from 1250 Vallejo Street, Suite 9, San Francisco, CA
94109. Trip cancellation insurance is recommended,
especially if you are buying discount tickets. The
Consumer Reports Travel Letter examined this subject
thoroughly in its January 1989 issue, available for $5 from
CRTL, 2506 Washington Street, Mt. Vernon, NY 10553.

Make your reservations as far in advance as possible,
especially if traveling in the high season from November
through February. Wherever feasible, make your hotel
reservations as well. This is a must if you plan to go in
December or January.

Traveling within Thailand

This itinerary calls for traveling by air between the main
destinations within Thailand, both to save time and
because fares are reasonable. Ground transportation in
Thailand is relatively reliable and efficient, but the distances involved between the three major areas covered in
this book are best managed by air. Thai Airways controls
the vast majority of key domestic routes within the country, although Bangkok Airways has initiated service to a
few of the more popular destinations. As with most facilities that deal with the public in Thailand, the airline services are prompt and courteous.

There are regular flights between Bangkok and nearly
two dozen domestic destinations. Daily direct service is
available to Chiang Mai, Chiang Rai, Phuket, and Koh
Samui. In the north, there are several daily flights
between Chiang Mai and Chiang Rai and between Chiang
Mai and Mae Hong Son. Fares average between $15 and

$75 one-way from one city to another. Reservations can
be made by U.S. travel agents (advisable if you are traveling in the high season) or in Bangkok. Thai Airways
has many locations in Bangkok, including the Don
Muang International Airport: the head office is at 89
Vibhavadi Rangsit Road, Bangkok 10900, tel. (02) 513-
0121. The reservation address for Bangkok Airways is
144 Sukhumvit Road, Bangkok 10110, tel. (02) 253-4014.
There is regular and efficient bus and railroad service to
the north and south of Thailand as well. Complete
schedules are available from the Tourist Authority of
Thailand.

We do not recommend driving a car in Thailand.
Although the farther you are from Bangkok, the safer it
feels, it is easy to get lost, and local driving habits are
erratic. Motorbike rentals, however, are fun and convenient in the north and south, if you are experienced and
confident. If you plan to do any driving, it is advisable
to acquire an International Driving Permit before you
leave the United States. (They cost $5, require two cur-
rent passport-size photos, and are available through the
Automobile Association of America.)

Bangkok has a highly developed transportation system of buses, taxis, and three-wheeled motorized *sam-
lors* called "*tuk-tuks.*" Only the buses have set fares, but
the taxis and tuk-tuks are so abundant, convenient, and
relatively inexpensive (as long as you bargain hard) that
you will probably choose to use them for your city travel in Bangkok and Chiang Mai as well. In Chiang Mai
and southern Thailand, a common option is the *songthaew*, a small pickup truck converted into a taxi with
padded benches in the covered bed. Some are public
with set fares, as on Koh Samui. Some in Chiang Mai are
privately operated and subject to negotiation, with prices
falling between the low end of the tuk-tuk and the high
end of the private car. Chiang Rai still has genuine sam-
lors, manually powered pedicabs, useful for short jaunts
around town.

Most of the itinerary suggestions include self-guided tours of the sightseeing highlights. But since Bangkok is so big and so potentially overwhelming, we have found it useful, for reasons of timing and easier transportation, to join certain organized day excursions that cover the outlying areas—notably Damnoen Saduak and Ayutthaya. In the hill country of Chiang Mai, Chiang Rai, and Mae Hong Son, unless you are an experienced hiker in foreign terrain, it is advisable to trek with local operators who know the territory.

As you move from one region to the next within Thailand, check the weather forecasts in the Thai newspapers, the Bangkok *Post* or *The Nation*. There's no sense getting caught in a monsoon that you can avoid. You might also supplement this itinerary with good local maps—Nancy Chandler's city maps of Bangkok and Chiang Mai are colorful, detailed, hand-drawn, and opinionated. Other maps, including useful bus route maps, are available from the Tourist Authority of Thailand.

Safety in Thailand

Although Bangkok has a reputation as a haven for illicit activity, and in certain areas that reputation holds true, Thailand as a whole is a very safe country for the independent traveler. Stories of theft and coercion center around the notorious Patpong District, and travelers are forewarned to tread cautiously in that "red-light" area. We have also heard stories of petty theft in inadequately secured beach bungalows, ransacked or stolen luggage on overnight bus rides, and such valuables as cameras, radios, and jewelry being "borrowed indefinitely." But those accounts are the exceptions. While it is always wise to be prudent about your possessions and to take advantage of hotel safes for storing your passport, airline tickets, and traveler's checks, you will feel safe and secure in most areas of Thailand.

Money

Throughout this book, prices are quoted in the local Thai currency, *baht*, followed in parentheses by the approximate U.S. dollar values. All prices are subject to change, of course, and they usually go up, due to inflation. But the exchange rate in Thailand has been very stable at about 25.3 baht to $1, or 1 baht = $0.04. When confronted with the baht price, it is easy to calculate the conversion in your head by either dividing by 25 or multiplying by four and moving the decimal two places to the left; for example, 75 baht (the price of a top-end curry dish in a moderate restaurant) equals about $3. Carry a well-known brand of traveler's checks that can easily be exchanged (for a higher rate than cash) at hotels and banks. Larger establishments also accept major credit cards.

All the prices and admissions quoted here are approximate, subject to relative increases or drops according to currency fluctuations and inflation.

Lodging

Thai people are very service oriented, and you will be greeted with exceptional hospitality no matter what price you pay for your accommodations. Almost all midrange to luxury hotels ($30-$300) are furnished with Western amenities, including Western flush toilets and hot water baths and showers. At the budget end, in the inexpensive dormitories and bungalows ($2-$10), you are likely to find Asian-style floor toilets and traditional bucket showers with cold water. If you plan to trek or stay overnight on a remote beach, be prepared with your own towels and toilet paper and count on outside plumbing.

Food

As you will discover throughout the country, Thai cooking is a source of pride and wonder. While presentation varies from simple plastic bowls at sidewalk stands to decorated china and artistic displays in the finer restaurants, the sources of Thai culinary magic are consistent.

Cooks use fresh, exotic ingredients and combine them in
traditional but often highly personalized styles. Even if
you have trained your palate in Thai restaurants in the
states, you may be surprised by the complexity of tastes
and the degree of spiciness in the indigenous dishes.
You will never be bored. Indeed, you will often wonder
how your next meal could possibly top the one you just
finished. Expect to pay about $3 to $8 for a full, satisfy-
ing meal. You can spend more: up to $20 or $30 per person in the biggest restaurants and top-flight hotels. But
Thai food need not be pricey to be excellent.

Visas
A valid passport is necessary for entry into Thailand, and
a tourist visa is required for stays of more than 15 days.
You can make your trip without a visa, but upon exit
you must pay a penalty of 100 baht ($4) per day for
every day over the limit. In the United States, you can
obtain applications and process your visa through the
Thai consulate in Washington, D.C. It is often more convenient to use a visa service. For a small fee, the service
company will handle the paperwork quickly and effi-
ciently. Visas Unlimited (703 Market Street, Suite 802, San
Francisco, CA 94103; tel. 415-495-5216), and Visa Aides
(870 Market Street, San Francisco, CA 94105; tel. 415-362-
7137) are all recommended.

When to Go
Thailand's weather pattern falls into three seasons: "cool"
(actually warm and dry) from October through February
(temperatures from 75 to 90 degrees, coolest in
December and January); hot and dry from March through
May (with temperatures sometimes climbing above 100
degrees); and rainy from June through September (with
the heaviest downpours in September). "Hot" means temperatures sometimes topping 100 degrees. "Rainy" does
not necessarily mean constant or torrential downpours.
Drenching storms can come and go in bursts, separated

by warm, sunny stretches. The wettest month is September; fall monsoons in the south can inhibit travel. The most popular time for travel to Thailand is November through January, coinciding with the mildest weather and an abundance of national holidays and regional festivals. Traveling in the off-seasons, especially in late September and early October, can be especially pleasant—without so many tourists around—and economical: many hotels, resorts, and guest houses offer "low" season discounts, up to 20 percent, on room rates.

The king's birthday, December 5, is cause for celebration throughout the country, with many special events in Bangkok. Visakha Puja Day, marking the birth, enlightenment, and death of Buddha, is a national public holiday marked by candlelight temple processions. It falls on the full moon of the sixth lunar month, usually around the end of May. The traditional Thai New Year, Songkran, is celebrated April 13-15 with religious merit making, parades, and water throwing. One of the most colorful national festivals is Loi Krathong, on the full moon of the twelfth lunar month, usually mid-November. After sunset, people parade to the nearest body of water and launch flotillas of lotus-shaped banana leaf boats, honoring the water spirits and washing away the year's previous sins. The celebration is especially spectacular in Bangkok.

Special festivals also abound in the regions described in this itinerary. Songkran reaches grand proportions in Chiang Mai. In early February, that city holds a Flower Festival, featuring floral displays, floats, and beauty contests. In nearby Nan, the annual Lanna Boat Races take place in early October. In southern Thailand, many of the biggest festivals take place in Phuket, the major tourist island of the western coast. The Seafood Festival is held in late April and the Vegetarian Festival in mid-October. Surat Thani, on the eastern side of the isthmus, is the site of the Buddhist Chak Phra Festival in late October. Other notable festivals around Thailand include the mid-November Elephant Roundup in Surin, the late-July

Candle Festival in Ubon Ratchathani, the early-May
Rocket Festival in Yasothon, the Chon Buri Buffalo Races
every October, and the Chantaburi Fruits Fair in June.

Health Precautions

Consult your physician for advice on vaccinations, immun-
izations, and other precautions, especially against malaria
and hepatitis but also venereal diseases, cholera, and
typhoid fever. Malaria poses a decreasing risk, but disease-
carrying mosquitoes are said to be showing resistance to
the most common antimalarial drugs. Carry an effective
repellent (Avon bath oil works well), and don't forget to
apply it to your ankles, face, and neck, especially at dusk.
In mosquito areas of the rural north, consider sleeping
under a mosquito net or fan. Your doctor might suggest
taking medicines for treating colds and diarrhea as well.

Preventive medicine is always a good idea when traveling. We always drink bottled water, beer, wine, and soft
drinks instead of tap water. We also avoid unpeeled fruits
and vegetables, stay away from most uncooked foods, and
stick to freshly prepared foods at street stalls.

What to Pack

Travel light! If you are able to take only carryon baggage,
you will dramatically reduce the time spent at check-in
and customs counters. You will also minimize the possi-
bility of delayed or lost luggage and make it much easier
on yourself to move from plane to taxi, taxi to hotel, and
city to city. Never check anything you can't travel without (glasses, medicines, credit cards, traveler's checks,
address book), and consider carrying your passport, airline tickets, and traveler's checks in a money belt.
Photocopy your passport and the first page of each airline ticket and pack the copies separately. Remember to
take such travel amenities as an alarm clock, small flash-
light, binoculars, sleep mask, ear plugs, and reading
material. And while most pharmaceuticals and sundries
are available in Thailand, bring your own ointments

(antibacterial and antifungal), prescription drugs, vitamins, Band-Aids, sunscreen, and insect repellent.

Clothing

No matter which season you choose for your trip to Thailand, all you'll need are a few changes of lightweight, comfortable clothing. What you wear on the airplane will probably be suitable for most hotels and restaurants and warm enough for all regions (except the northern hills in the winter months, when you'll need a sweater or light jacket). Take light, cotton clothing that dries quickly and a pair of all-purpose walking shoes. Women can buy sarongs to use as a skirt, but pants are considered acceptable dress. Include shorts and a swimming suit but remember to cover up to prevent sunburn. Sandals or thongs are good for the beach. Dark glasses are highly recommended. A small, portable umbrella is useful in the rainy season or for fair-skinned travelers who need protection from the full sun. Don't overpack. You can always buy additional good quality, inexpensive clothing along the way throughout Thailand, especially in Bangkok and at the Chiang Mai night bazaar.

Recommended Reading

Many of the most informative studies of Thailand's history and culture are published only in Thailand, notably by Siam Society and DK Books in Bangkok. Readily available in the West are William Warren's books, including a study of silk magnate Jim Thompson, *The Legendary American* (Boston: Houghton Mifflin); *Bangkok* (with Marc Riboud) (New York: Weatherhill); a splendid photo essay, *Thailand: Seven Days in the Kingdom* (Singapore: Times Editions); and his excellent study of architecture and interior design, *Thai Style* (New York: Rizzoli). John Hoskin's *Chiang Mai and North Thailand* (Hong Kong: Hong Kong Publishing Company) is a good introduction to that area. *The Taste of Thailand* (New York: Macmillan) by chef Vatcharin Bhumichitr is a superb primer on Thai cuisine, with helpful historical and cultural overviews. *Insight Guide Thailand* (Singapore: APA Productions [HK], Ltd.) contains good historical synopses and descriptions of regional culture and society.

Tourist Board
Tourist Authority of Thailand, 3440 Wilshire Boulevard, Suite 1101, Los Angeles, CA 90010; tel. 213-382-2353.

DAY 1 Depart for Bangkok, Thailand's capital, biggest city and boiling caldron of past and present culture. Check into your hotel and savor your first genuine Thai meal in one of Bangkok's superb restaurants.

DAY 2 Explore some of Bangkok's many temples, starting with the spectacular Grand Palace. Learn about the history of Thailand's Buddhism and meet present-day practitioners of that ancient but still vital religion.

DAY 3 Experience the way Thai people have conducted commerce on their waterways by visiting the colorful Floating Market at Damnoen Saduak, where fruits and vegetables are sold from small boats. And discover the ancient seat of Thai Buddhism at Nakhon Pathom, site of the world's tallest Buddhist monument. Also visit the infamous Bridge on the River Kwai.

DAY 4 An air-conditioned bus ride to the ancient capital of Ayutthaya takes you back several centuries in Thailand's history and includes a stop at the resplendent Bang Pa-In summer palace. On your luxurious ride back to Bangkok aboard the *Oriental Queen*, you'll enjoy a delicious Thai buffet while cruising the Chao Phrya River.

ITINERARY OPTION: SUKHOTHAI

ITINERARY OPTION: THE NORTHEAST, NONG KHAI

DAY 5 A 1½-hour flight from Bangkok to Chiang Rai takes you into the heart of northern Thailand's hill country. Check into your guest house or hotel and begin to explore this provincial hub of trekking. Experience your first taste of the distinctive northern cuisine.

DAY 6 Explore the temples of Chiang Rai, take your time browsing through the shops overflowing with handicrafts from Thailand, Myanmar (Burma), and Laos, or negotiate your own excursion to ride elephants, swim in mountain streams under waterfalls, or visit a hill tribe village.

DAY 7 Today you'll drive to Thailand's northernmost point, the small town of Mae Sai at the Myanmar (Burmese) border, a focal point of many handicrafts, including delicately carved jade. Your drive will take you west to the legendary Golden Triangle, where Thailand, Myanmar, and Laos come together at the Mekong River, and then to the ancient capital of Chiang Saen.

ITINERARY OPTION: TREKKING

DAY 8 After a half-hour plane ride from Chiang Rai, you land in Thailand's second-largest city, Chiang Mai. Check into your hotel or guest house, and begin to explore this northern center of Thai handicrafts. You'll get your first glimpse of the fascinating Night Bazaar and savor a traditional Khantoke dinner.

DAY 9 Explore the old walled city and the historic temples of Chiang Mai, including Wat Chiang Man, Wat Phra Singh, and Wat Phrathat. Tour handicrafts workshops where lacquerware, wood carvings, umbrellas, jewelry, and celadon pottery are made. Ride up to Doi Suthep and investigate the golden "temple on the mountain." After dinner in one of Chiang Mai's enticing restaurants, reimmerse yourself in the carnival atmosphere of the night market.

DAY 10 The plane flight to Mae Hong Son takes only 45 minutes, but you suddenly find yourself light-years away from even the tempered civilizaton of Chiang Mai, surrounded by misty, jungle-clad hills. Choose an inexpensive bungalow in town or a quiet resort on the Ping River and settle into the peaceful pace of this northwestern outpost.

DAY 11 Rise before sunrise to catch the morning market, where hill tribe people and town dwellers lay out fish, fruit, vegetables, meat, and handicrafts for sale. You'll be one of only a handful of Westerners among these predawn traders. Walk, rent a motorbike, or hire a driver and ride up to the temple on the hill. Investigate the many trekking options for your next two days.

DAY 12 Trek through the hill country near the Myanmar border, exploring the jungle, fording streams, riding elephants, and eating and sleeping in hospitable tribal villages.

DAY 13 Continue your trek, meeting other ethnic tribal peoples of the north and discovering the rich and varied wildlife in the lush jungles and mountains. Alternatively, you can relax at your resort or continue to explore the immediate outskirts or the handicraft shops of town.

DAY 14 Your early afternoon flight will take you to Bangkok where you will switch planes for the southern island paradise of Koh Samui on the Gulf of Thailand. Check into an inexpensive beachside bungalow and enjoy a quick dip in the warm Gulf waters before a leisurely dinner overlooking the surf.

DAY 15 Use this day for R and R on the white sand beaches of Koh Samui, sunbathing, swimming and snorkeling, or exploring such island landmarks as the Big Buddha at Hin Ngu Temple, the Grandmother and Grandfather Rocks, and the interior waterfalls at Namuang and Hin Lad.

DAY 16 Take an excursion to the more remote and less touristed islands of Koh Phangan and Koh Tao, where accommodations and life are even simpler than on Koh Samui.

DAY 17 An early morning express boat from Koh Phangan or Koh Samui carries you past bizarre limestone formations to the mainland town of Surat Thani, where you catch an air-conditioned bus for the late morning ride across to the eastern coast of southern Thailand and the intriguing port of Krabi. After lunch in town, check into a bungalow on picturesque Phra Nang Bay. Dine on fresh seafood from the Andaman Sea.

DAY 18 Today you explore the natural and historical attractions of Krabi Province, including the 75-million-year-old Susan Hoi Shell Cemetery near Ban Laem Pho, the Tiger Cave Monastery, the Ao Luk and Sra-Yuan Thong caves, the Botanical Garden and National Park, or Poda Island.

DAY 19 A relaxing two-hour boat ride takes you to Koh Phi Phi, a breathtakingly beautiful pair of islands midway between Krabi and the large, popular resort island of Phuket. Check into a bungalow on Don Sai Beach and spend the afternoon sunning, swimming, or snorkeling. In the evening, after the boats have brought in the day's catch, try your favorite fish, crab, lobster, or prawns hot off the barbecue grill.

DAY 20 Take a long-tail boat to Phi Phi Le, the uninhabited twin to Phi Phi Don, and see the huge cave where locals climb rickety bamboo ladders to gather swallows' nests for bird's nest soup. Schedule a snorkeling or scuba diving excursion to one of the coral reefs in the pristine waters.

DAY 21 Your morning boat ride from Koh Phi Phi takes you to Phuket in time to make an early afternoon flight back for one more evening in Bangkok, where you can try a new restaurant, enjoy a drink on the terrace of the Oriental or Shangri-la Hotel, sample the nightlife, or catch up on shopping.

DAY 22 There is always one more thing you'll want to do before you leave Bangkok, and this is your chance. Visit a temple, palace, or park, tour the narrow *klongs* that run through the city, explore Chinatown, or shop for bargains and souvenirs. Before preparing for your departure home, treat yourself to a final, sumptuous meal of Thai cuisine.

UNITED STATES TO BANGKOK

Your trip starts with a long flight to Bangkok. Remember that you "lose" a day when your plane crosses the international date line. As you approach Bangkok, you sweep in over vast plains of rice fields that gradually merge into the urban sprawl. In the late afternoon or dusk you can spot the gleaming spires of ancient temples, signals of the rich culture you're about to enter. From the scramble at Don Muang Airport, you sink into a relaxed evening at your hotel.

Suggested Schedule	
Morning	Depart for Bangkok.
Late afternoon	Arrive at Don Muang International Airport.
5:00 p.m.	Clear immigration and customs.
5:30 p.m.	Taxi to hotel in Bangkok.
7:00 p.m.	Dinner.
8:00 p.m.	Early to bed.

Arrival
After immigration clearance, you will step into the appropriate customs line. If you have nothing to declare, there will be no wait. Downtown Bangkok is 22 km south of the airport. Bus and taxi service is available, taxis being by far the most convenient. As soon as you leave the customs area, you will be directed to the taxi counter, where transportation to your hotel will be quickly arranged. Change about $20 at the nearby bank desk. The set taxi fare for the 30-minute ride into downtown Bangkok is 300 baht ($12). You can leave the airport and bargain a private driver down to 150 or 200 baht ($6-$8), inquire about a minibus to your specific hotel, about 100

baht ($4), or experiment with the public buses if you have a good bus map; the fares are 5 to 15 baht ($0.20-$0.60). It is highly recommended that you arrive with a hotel reservation in Bangkok.

Also on arrival, you are likely to be approached by smiling young Thais who speak good English and welcome you to Thailand. They work for tour companies and will encourage you to sign up for packaged day trips. Although they are eager to sell, their friendliness is genuine, and they can be very helpful as sources of information, even if you aren't buying.

The taxi ride into town can be harrowing if your driver is one of those who mistakes the expressway for the Indianapolis 500. Most are excellent and safe drivers, but the traffic patterns in Bangkok are mad, including sudden passes, lane changes that can be breathtaking, and horrendous traffic jams at huge intersections with interminable stoplights. Once you arrive at your hotel, feel free to tip your driver (up to 10%, or keep dollar bills handy) or not, according to your estimation of the service.

Helpful Hints

Every time you set out for a destination in Bangkok, have someone write the name and address in Thai so you can show it to your taxi or tuk-tuk driver or to friendly people on the street. Throughout Thailand, in guidebooks and on maps and street signs, the English translations of Thai names vary greatly. For instance, you will find Bangkok's main river referred to as the Chao Phya, Chao Phraya, Chao Phrya, or Chao Prya. The spellings are phonetically based—"j" is often substituted for "tch," "d" for "t," "g" for "k," and "h's" and "r's" come and go without warning—so expect some confusion.

The Thai language is extremely difficult to master, but you will be well received if you learn a few civilities. To say "thank-you," men say "kawpkuhn krap" and women "kawpkuhn ka." (The same articles, "krap" and "ka," are added to most greetings and questions for politeness.) "Sawatii" serves as "hello," "good morning," and "good bye." "Yes" as a statement is "chai"; as agreement it is "krap" or "ka." "No" is "mai." You might want to remember "Puut thai mai dai," or "I cannot speak Thai." And one uniquely all-purpose Thai phrase is "mai pen rai," which is used as a verbal shrug for "never mind," "don't worry," "it really doesn't matter." It reflects the Buddhist-imbued relaxed attitude many Thais take toward the nonessential, transient nature of the material world.

Everywhere you will meet people who go out of their way to make you feel welcome. In return, you can observe a few simple customs. It is impolite to touch people, including children, on their heads or to sit with the soles of your feet pointing at another person. Buddhist monks are not allowed to touch and will some-times refrain from social contact with women. Losing one's temper is virtually taboo; it is always good to remember the axiom, *mai pen rai.*

Lodging

As the travel hub of Southeast Asia, Bangkok offers accommodations for every budget and taste, from the most minimal dormitory-style rooms to the splendor of grand hotels. The legendary jewel in the crown is the **Oriental Hotel** at 48 Oriental Avenue, Bangkok, 10500, perenially cited as one of the best hotels in the world. Its over-400 rooms are beautifully appointed, and the lavish-ly adorned hotel overlooks the Chao Phrya River. On the opposite side of the river sits the new **Oriental Spa**, a complete health and relaxation resort. The rates—6,000 to 65,000 baht ($240-$2,600)—reflect the Oriental's luxury and legendary status. Rooms vary from single and double rooms overlooking the river or garden to elaborate suites and the legendary Authors' Residence. Famous for its restaurants and Thai Cooking School, the Oriental deserves a visit and perhaps a cup of tea on the Riverside Terrace or the Verandah. Tel. 236-0500. Nearby on the river is the high-rise and equally luxurious **Shangri-La**, at 89 Soi Wat Suan Plu, New Road, Bangkok, 10500. Its 650 rooms and suites range from 5,200 to 45,000 baht ($208-$1,800). The Lobby Lounge is bedazzling, a fine place to treat yourself to an expensive drink at sunset. The **Hotel Siam-Intercontinental**, 967 Rama 1 Road, Bangkok, 10330, is a low-rise luxury hotel situated in a 26-acre park on the Srapatum Palace property, near Siam Square. Rooms are 4,600 to 18,000 baht ($184-$720).

You can have the convenient location of the Oriental and the Shangri-La—near the river and central shopping district—at nearly a tenth the price at the **Swan Hotel**, 31 Soi Charoenkrung, 36 New Road, Bangkok, 10500. This modest lodging, slightly funky and timeworn, is located directly behind the Oriental and is one of Bangkok's best deals at 700 baht ($28) for an air-conditioned double, tel. 234-8594. Our favorite reasonably priced hotel is the **Royal Hotel** at 2 Rajadamnern Avenue. Its location near the heart of Old Bangkok puts it within easy walking distance of the Grand Palace and Wat Pho. Its 300 rooms are clean and comfortable, the staff is helpful, and the large, remodeled, bustling lobby has a heady international atmosphere. Ask for a room away from the street. The 24-hour coffee shop serves a variety of Western and Thai dishes. Rates are 956 to 1,295 baht ($38-$52), tel. 222-9111. The **Boston Inn**, 4 Soi Si Bamphen, Rama IV Road, is popular with budget travelers for its cheap, clean rooms and friendly feeling. Dorm beds go for 60 baht, ($2.40), while rooms with private bath are 120 to 190 baht ($4.80-$7.60). Low-priced guest houses can be found in Banglamphu District along Khao San Road just north of the Democracy Monument. The **Peachy Guest House**, 10 Phra Arthit Road, for instance, charges only 140 baht ($5.60) for a double room with fan and shared bath. Others nearby include the **Nith Charoen Hotel**, 183 Khaosan Road, and the **Chart, Lek** and **P.S.** guest houses.

Food

Dining will undoubtedly be one of your most memorable activities in Thailand. Becoming the culinary rage the world over, Thai cuisine takes relatively simple ingredients—white rice (steamed or "sticky"), pork, beef, poultry, seafood, herbs, and spices—and creates soups and main course dishes that are amazingly complex. The most prevalent flavors come from chilies, coconut milk, garlic, coriander, lemongrass, fish sauce, lime leaves, basil, galangal, ginger, shallots, shrimp paste, tamarind, and turmeric. The sumptuous curries sometimes literally bring you to tears, especially when the fiery native chilies are used in abundance in conjunction with garlic and ginger.

Although Bangkok caters to every national taste, it would be a crime to ignore the superb native cooking available in every price range, from the thousands of street vendors to resplendent restaurants. Some of the common dishes include *gai tom ka* (chicken coconut soup), *tom yam gung* (hot and sour soup with prawns), *pad thai* (Thai fried noodles with various ingredients), *gaeng kiow wan* (green beef curry), *gaeng pet gai* (red chicken curry), *tod man pla* (fish cake), and literally hundreds of variations. A cornucopia of dessert sweets is concocted from eggs, beans, rice flour, roots, seeds, palm sugar, and coconut. And the selection of tropical Thai fruits is staggering. In addition to bananas, pineapples, oranges, mangoes, and papayas, you will discover an array of more exotic fruits. The sapodilla is plum-shaped, brown-skinned, and bears very sweet flesh. Beneath the thick, purple peel of the mangosteen lies a succulent, slightly tangy fruit meat. The rambutan is notable for its long red and green bristles encasing white, delicately perfumed flesh like the litchi. The large jackfruit is covered with thick, thorny skin and yields tangy yellow flesh. The pomelo looks like a big, pale green grapefruit but is less juicy and less tart. Durians are best known as "stinky fruit" for their surprisingly rank odor, but inside the thorny, yellowish brown shell is a very sweet, yellow-tinted flesh. The two most common Thai "apples," the rose apple and the custard apple, have little in common; the former is light pink with smooth skin and crisp meat, and the latter has a pale-green armored exterior, with sweet, white, segmented flesh and an abundance of inedible black seeds.

Such luxury hotels as the **Oriental**, the **Shangri-La**, and the **Siam-Intercontinental** offer fabulous and expensive spreads. The Seafood/Thai buffet lunch at the Siam-Intercontinental, however, is a real bargain at 135 baht ($5.40) per person for all you can eat of fresh prawns, crab, mussels, curries, noodles, soups, and salads. (Watch out for the markup on drinks, though.) Reservations are recommended, tel. 253-0355. **Bussaracum**, at 35 Soi Pipat 2, is famous for its individually prepared dishes and smooth service, at prices adding up to perhaps 500 baht ($20) per person. Reservations are advised, tel. 235-8915.

We've had some of our most splendid meals in the moderately priced restaurants. Our favorite is **Lemongrass**, 5/1 Sukhumvit Road. Soi 24. Dishes run about 75 baht ($3) each, and two people can eat and drink heartily for less than 250 baht ($10) each. Chef Narin Chotipanang and his partner, Vorachoon Yuchinda, oversee this cozy, side-street restaurant and prepare nearly 50 original versions of such dishes as *moo sarong* (minced pork wrapped in thread noodles and deep fried), *yam tau-poo* (winged-bean salad), *chuchi prik yuak sodsai* (stuffed mild green peppers with chili sauce), *gang ped* (green curry chicken), *moo pad kapi* (pork fried in shrimp paste), *masman nua* (mild curry of tender beef), *laab pla tu* (minced fish salad), *moo-o-cha* (mild dry curry pork), *dom ka gai sai hua blee-pao* (chicken with edible banana-flower and coconut cream), and fabulous arabica coffee in plunger-filter pots. The service, overseen by captain Daeng Takrudngam, is impeccable; tel. 258-8637. The **Silom Village Trade**

Center, 286 Silom Road, is a tourist shopping complex
of shops and boutiques, with excellent food tucked in
back. Avoid the formal restaurant and dinner show
upstairs; instead, try the patio restaurants that offer fresh
seafood and mouth-watering curries at reasonable prices.
For less than 400 baht ($16), two people can gorge on
dry beef curry, chicken-coconut milk soup, green and
red curry dishes, moo sarong, fried crab legs, and other
tempting delicacies. **D'jit Pochana**, with three locations—60 Sukhumvit Soi 20, 1082 Paholyotin Road, and
23/368-380 Paholyotin Road—is deservedly famous for its
reasonably priced Thai dishes and pleasant atmosphere.
The Oriental Hotel took over the former D'jit Pochana II
on the opposite bank of the Chao Phrya from the hotel
and renamed it **Rim Naam Terrace**. A wide variety of
soups, appetizers, seafood dishes, and favorites like
spiced salad of minced pork, shredded sun-dried and
honeyed beef, red and green curries, plus enticing Thai
desserts are served in a beautiful riverside setting. Dishes
are priced in the 80 to 150 baht ($3.20-$6) range. Take
the free shuttle ferry from the dock at the Oriental Hotel.
Vijit, at the corner of Rajadamnern Avenue and
Prachathiptai, near the Democracy Monument, is popular
with civil servants and office workers from the surrounding offices but essentially undiscovered by foreigners. It
is noisy at night when the musical combo cranks up its
pop music. But the chili oil prawns and garlic, the chick-
en curry, and other dishes are more than worth the clam-
or. This a real taste of Bangkok, without touristy trappings. The **Whole Earth Restaurant**, at 93/3 Soi
Langsuan, Ploenchit Road, is more conscious of Western
clientele, serving vegetarian dishes at around 70 baht
($2.80) each for lunch, plus a wide range of beautifully
prepared nonvegetarian soups and curries. One afternoon, looking for a fast lunch, we slipped into the **Sky-
High Restaurant**, around the corner from the Royal
Hotel. It may have looked like a run-of-the-mill coffee
shop, but we were served an extraordinary charcoal-fired

pot of hot and sour prawn soup for 140 baht ($5.60), indicative of the delicious, individually prepared dishes available all over the city. Recently remodeled with clean chrome and mirrors, Sky-High is an especially pleasant spot for a quick breakfast or lunch, but it has a full menu for dinner, too.

There are many more famous and *farang* (Westerner)-oriented restaurants in Bangkok, such as the increasingly popular **Cabbages & Condoms**, operated by the Thai Population Development Association at 10 Soi 12 Sukhumvit Road, but you will have a hard time finding budget dining in such a pleasant setting as the **Kaloang Home Kitchen**. Then again, you may have a hard time finding this riverside, open-air restaurant tucked into a neighborhood at the end of Sri Ayutthaya just past the National Library. Your best bet is to have someone write the name and address in Thai for your driver. A full range of Thai dishes, many quite spicy, is offered—curries, fish dishes, chicken, salads—and small long-tail boats cruise up to the dock and sell dried squid, reconstituted on a charcoal grill. Go in the late afternoon as the sun is setting and enjoy the view of boats moving up and down the river, birds flitting around the piers and bushes, and a genuinely downhome atmosphere for less than 150 baht ($6) per person. It's a real and surprisingly tranquil Bangkok experience. The address is 2 Sri Ayutthaya; tel. 281-9228.

If you have a cast-iron stomach and a sense of adventure, you can try eating from **street corner carts**. This is where thousands of Thais take breakfast, lunch, or dinner daily, digging into bowls of noodles with broths and ingredients added on the spot. But unless you feel comfortable just pointing at the things you want added (and some are mysterious-looking indeed), you should probably ask a local resident for advice on how to order.

Taxis and Tuk-Tuks

Getting around Bangkok is easy once you adapt to bargaining for a price with taxi and tuk-tuk drivers. None of
the vehicles are metered, so it's up to you to negotiate
before you get in. The tuk-tuks are noisy and you suck in
a lot of the horrendous traffic fumes that pervade
Bangkok, especially if you're stuck behind a bus, but
they are still the most enjoyable way to ride. Their owners proudly paint them and dress them up with colored
lights. Zipping through the crowded streets and back
alleys can be like a carnival ride. Short trips should cost
only 30 to 60 baht ($1.20-$2.40) and longer rides 70 to
100 baht ($2.80-$4). You might feel safer enclosed in an
air-conditioned taxi, but you will pay at least twice as
much for the same distances. Fares don't get much lower
than about 80 baht ($3.20) around town and 200 baht
($8) to the airport. Many drivers know a little English and
love to try it out in conversation. Some will offer to come
back for you to complete your round-trip or arrange to
drive you the next day.

Helpful Hints

Before leaving a hotel, restaurant, or public building, ask
a local what it should cost for a taxi or tuk-tuk to your
next destination. They will give you the current range for
tourists, usually saying, "Don't pay more than...." Heed
their advice and bargain hard. Only rarely will a driver
refuse your top price, and even then another is usually
nearby.

BANGKOK: CITY OF ANGELS

Bangkok suffers all the ills of a modern metropolis, but it is also a gilded city of canals, temples, and reclining Buddhas, the kind of place you'd expect to find at the end of a yellow brick road. Today, by guiding yourself through some of Bangkok's most significant temples, you will get an overview of this society shaped by Siamese kings and Buddhist priests.

Suggested Schedule

7:00 a.m.	Breakfast at your hotel.
8:30 a.m.	Grand Palace and temple tour.
12:00 noon	Lunch.
1:30 p.m.	Continue your tour of Bangkok's temples.
7:00 p.m.	Dinner.

Bangkok

The greater metropolitan area of Thailand's largest city covers 580 square miles and is home to over 6 million people, about one-tenth of the entire country's population. Bangkok's contradictory potpourri of ancient temples and high-rise hotels, quiet canals and frantic expressways, abject poverty and middle-class affluence, tranquil saffron-robed monks and hustling tuk-tuk drivers is enough to warrant its reputation as the most exotic city in Asia. Since King Rama I made it the country's capital in the late eighteenth century, Bangkok has grown into a city that is at once magnificent and mad. The old "Venice of the East," with a maze of canals (*klongs*) supporting fishermen and floating markets, is now traversed by bustling avenues carrying 90 percent of Thailand's automobile traffic. You can look up from the congested streets to the sharply curving spires of an ancient temple and understand why the Thais call their capital city the "City of Angels," or Krungthep, shortened from Krung

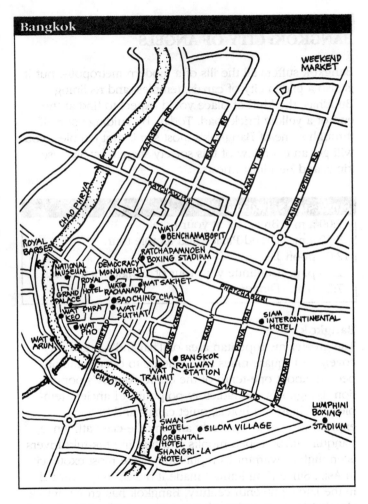

Thep Manakhon Bovorn Ratanakosin Mahintharayutthaya Mahadilokpop Noparatratchathani Burirom Udomratchani-vetmahasathan Avatarnsathit Sakkathattiyavisnukarmarasit. You can walk alongside a polluted klong and be nearly overcome by the stench of automobile exhaust and sewage, then slip into a sidewalk café, dip into a spicy seafood soup or a hot chicken curry, and be transported into a paradise of exotic aromas and flavors.

The vision of King Rama I was to build Bangkok in the image of Ayutthaya, the old capital that had been ravaged by the Burmese invaders in 1767. He reclaimed a swampy village on the banks of the Chao Phrya River, importing Ayutthayan artisans and calling for the construction of canals to resemble the Ayutthaya pattern. Bangkok relied primarily on water transportation for nearly two hundred years, even when trade with the West started booming in the late nineteenth century under King Mongkut. Road construction advanced dramatically only after World War II. Since the mid-1960s, especially after the influx of U.S. troops, migration into the capital from the rural countryside has put enormous population pressures on Bangkok. Thirty years ago, only 1.5 million people lived in the city; now there are at least one million cars.

Bangkok proper is bordered by the curving Chao Phrya River on the west. The Old Royal City runs alongside the water, across the river from Thonburi. The Dusit area, with the new Royal Palace, government buildings, and zoo developed under King Rama V, is just to the northeast of the Old Royal City, across the Klong Phadung. "Modern" Bangkok, where you find many of the new hotels, towering office buildings, and exclusive shops, extends to the south and east, along New Petchburi, Sukhumvit, and Silom roads. The combination of Western influences and Asian tradition, and the imposition of helter-skelter modern development on an ancient culture that in many ways is still thriving, makes Bangkok wild, foreboding, enticing, exciting, and endlessly intriguing.

Travel Route
From the Royal Hotel, turn left (south) down Rachini Road (on the far side of the canal). At Bamrung Muang Road, turn right (west), and at the end of the block you will see the tall white walls of the Grand Palace. The entrance is around to the right on Naphralan Road.

From the Oriental, Shangri-La, or Swan Hotel, take a bus, taxi, or tuk-tuk to the Grand Palace. Or catch an express river taxi from the Oriental pier and ride up the Chao Phrya River to the dock near Naphralan Road. Fares start at 3 baht ($0.12). The Grand Palace is straight ahead as you exit the pier.

Upon leaving the Grand Palace, turn left (west) and walk along Naphralan Road, turning left (south) again on Maharaj Road. Walk along the west wall of the Grand Palace grounds until you reach Charoen Krung Road. Turn left (east). The entrance to Wat Pho is in the middle of the block. Return to your hotel or ride to a restaurant via tuk-tuk; there are always several waiting outside the temples. In the afternoon, hire a tuk-tuk to take you to the remaining sites and temples.

Sightseeing Highlights
▲▲▲Grand Palace—Here is the one sight that best captures the checkered history, royal splendor, and religious symbolism of premodern Bangkok. Construction on the sprawling grounds was initiated by King Rama I when he moved the country's capital to Bangkok in 1782. Rama I, known previously as General Chao Phrya Chakri, established the royal dynasty that has endured to the present after the long succession of kingdoms, including the great Ayutthaya era in the seventeenth century, that had marked Thai history. Under the Chakri dynasty, Thai authority extended north to the Golden Triangle and south into the narrow isthmus between the Gulf of Thailand and the Andaman Sea. Foreign trade flourished in the mid-1800s, but unlike all of its neighbors, Siam was never governed by an imperial power, and the history of political independence and cultural integrity are important factors in preserving Thailand's unique character. Western ideas of politics and economy nonetheless seeped into the nation, especially under the reigns of King Mongkut and his son King Chulalongkorn. In 1932, a bloodless coup, the first of many throughout

the twentieth century, led to the establishment of a constitutional monarchy, governed by a prime minister but strongly shaped by the military. Today, Thailand's constitutional monarchy, designed along the lines of the United Kingdom's government, is presided over by King Bhumibol Adulyadej, ninth king of the Chakri dynasty and the country's longest-reigning monarch. He is chief of state, with an executive branch Council of Ministers, head of the armed forces, and Upholder of the Buddhist Religion. Legislative power is held by the National Assembly, comprising a popularly elected Parliament and an executive-appointed Senate. King Bhumibol Adulyadej was born in Cambridge, Massachusetts, on December 5, 1927, and educated in Bangkok and Switzerland, assuming the throne in 1946 upon the death of his elder brother. The Royal Family, including Queen Sirikit and their four children, are subjects of semidivine worship in Thailand, and visitors are expected to accord them the greatest respect.

The Grand Palace compound embodies much of Thailand's history. It includes the Palace buildings, a model of the magnificent Khmer temple, Angkor Wat, and the spectacular Temple of the Emerald Buddha. Among the royal buildings are the Chakri Maha Prasat, British-designed royal residence built for Rama V. It features an Italianate facade and a three-tiered Thai roof. The Dusit Maha Prasat, or audience hall, was built under Rama I in 1789. Next door is the Aphon Phimok Pavilion, or king's "disrobing pavilion." There are guides at the entrance offering their services for about 450 baht ($18). You can bargain down to half that price or less or very easily tour the grounds yourself with the pamphlet provided at the gate. Just inside the entrance you will find a small museum—the Royal Coins and Medals Pavilion—with a collection of artifacts, mostly having to do with royal military activities from various periods in the country's history. Other sites on the grounds include the Forbidden Quarters, used in the past to house the king's wives; the Borompiman Hall, once the residence of the crown prince who became King Rama VI; and the Amrin Vinichai Hall, a gorgeously painted audience hall originally built by Rama I and still used for special ceremonies such as coronations. The Grand Palace is open daily 8:30 to 11:30 a.m. and 1:00 to 3:30 p.m. Admission is 125 baht ($5).

▲▲▲**Wat Phra Keo**—Located in the Grand Palace complex, the Temple of the Emerald Buddha is deservedly one of Bangkok's two most famous temples—in a city with more than 400. Rama I built this remarkable chapel to enshrine the legendary Emerald Buddha image brought down from northern Siam. The image, actually carved from jasper, was discovered in Chiang Rai in 1434, when lightning cracked open an old *chedi* (a reliquary tower, often referred to as a stupa, typically bell shaped and tapering to a spire, and built to enshrine Buddha relics or the ashes of notable persons). The Emerald Buddha stands less than two-and-a-half feet high but commands a lofty position within the temple, enthroned in a towering altar. From just outside the temple doors, the view of the Buddha image is almost other-worldly, and it is only from here that you are allowed to take pictures; no photographs are allowed inside the temple. With the turning of each of Thailand's three seasons, the king ascends the altar and changes the statue's costumes. Nearly over-shadowed by the gloriously detailed chapel, which features reflecting glass chips, blue tile, and great interior murals of the *Ramakien* (the Thai version of India's Ramayana story), it nonetheless remains the most sacred of the country's Buddha images.

▲▲▲**Wat Pho**—The oldest temple-monastery complex in Bangkok, Wat Pho is most famous for the immense Reclining Buddha. Also known as Wat Phra Chetupon, its grounds are a maze of chapels, pavilions, Buddha images, chedis, and marble reliefs. In keeping with the role of the early temples as institutions of education as well as worship, many of the objects and paintings were originally installed at Wat Pho for the edification of the public, without any explicit connection to religion. Hence the temple has been known informally as Thailand's first university. Buildings and chedis were constructed here over the course of four centuries. The complex is fascinating but little prepares you for what you see when you enter the sixteenth century Temple of the Reclining Buddha. Taking up nearly the entire structure, the figure of Buddha lying on his side is 145 feet long and 50 feet high. Built of plaster-covered brick, the Buddha is plated with gold leaf. The soles of its feet are inlaid with 108 mother-of-pearl images of the auspicious signs of Buddha. The temple was enlarged and remodeled in 1789 by Rama I and has been undergoing constant reconstruction and repair in recent years. Around the grounds are many souvenir stands and stalls where visitors can make offerings to help support the renovations. In return, a monk might hang a small Buddha image amulet around your neck or tie a *sai sin* around your wrist. This thin piece of orange cotton cord has been blessed by the monks and is believed to provide protection from evil spirits. Wat Pho is open daily 8:00 a.m. to 5:00 p.m. Admission is 15 baht ($0.60).

▲▲**National Museum**—Reputed to be the largest museum in Southeast Asia, the National Museum offers a fine beginner's introduction to the art and culture of old Siam and contemporary Thailand. The exhibit rooms are organized to represent the main eras of artistic development: Dvaravati (6th C.–11th C.); Srivichaya (8th C.–13th C.); Lop Buri or Khmer (11th C.–14th C.); Chiang Saen (12th C.–20th C.); Sukhothai (13th C.–15th C.); Ayutthaya (15th C.–18th C.); and Bangkok or Ratanakosin (late 18th C. to the present). Many of the exhibits of artifacts, sculptures, and Buddha images are stunning. Occupying a section of the old Palace of the Front, the museum comprises several significant buildings, including the Isarawinitchai Hall (a former audience hall), the Manghalaphisak Pavilion, the elegant wooden Red House (exhibiting furniture of

the early monarchs), and the Phutthaisawan Chapel, built
in 1787 at the dawn of the Bangkok period to house the
Phra Buddha Sihing, a beloved bronze Sukhothai Buddha
image. Guided tours through the exhibits are available on
Tuesday, Wednesday, and Thursday, with lectures focus-
ing on significant aspects of painting, sculpture, architecture, and Thai Buddhism. The museum is located next to
Thamasat University on Na Prathat Road and is open 9:00
a.m. to 4:00 p.m. every day except Monday and Tuesday.
Admission is 25 baht ($1), free on Saturday and Sunday.

▲▲▲**Wat Sakhet**—King Rama III dreamed up the idea
of reproducing an artificial hill that had been a feature of
the ancient capital, Ayutthaya. Bangkok's soft earth
would not easily support such a project, however, and it
was not completed until the reign of Rama V near the
end of the nineteenth century. A circular stairway of 318
steps winds up "The Golden Mount" from the old Wat
Sakhet. Along the way, you can see the walls, altars, and
images that have twisted and turned as the soft ground
shifted over time. At the top, 78 meters from street level,
you get one of the best panoramic views of Bangkok.
Admission to the hilltop temple is 5 baht ($0.20). Wat
Sakhet is also the site of a festive temple fair every
November. It is located southeast of the big intersection
of Damrong Rak, Rajadamnern Avenue, and Mahachai
Road.

▲▲**Wat Rachanada**—Although this wat is unspectacular
by Bangkok standards, it houses a fascinating amulet
market. The Buddhist amulets are small terra-cotta or
metal charms, often encased in plastic, which are worn
on a gold or silver chain around the neck. They are
believed to have great protective and attractive powers.
In addition to amulets, the complex of stalls has displays
of various Buddha images, phallic stones, spirit houses,
carved elephants, and other auspicious symbols. The
market is inside the temple walls, across the klong and
Mahachai Road from Wat Sakhet.

▲▲**Wat Suthat**—Built in the early 1800s, this temple is notable both for its large *bot* (ordination hall) and *viharn* (daily services hall housing sacred objects) and for its elaborate murals. The collection of Buddha images housed here includes the huge Phra Buddha Chakymuni from fourteenth-century Sukhothai, brought to Bangkok by King Rama I. Immense, intricately carved doors from the reign of Rama II and fine murals from that of Rama III are also impressive.

▲▲**Giant Swing**—Two towering red poles, connected at the top by an ornately carved beam, can be seen just across the street from Wat Suthat. This is Sao Ching Cha, or the Giant Swing, once used during Brahman festivals to celebrate the annual earthly visit of the god Shiva. The ritual involved teams of young Brahmans swinging in great arcs to heights of 25 meters while trying to secure sacks of gold in their teeth. The dangerous exercise was banned in 1935.

▲▲▲**Wat Benchamabopit**—This beautifully designed royal temple is one of the best examples of how the Thai architectural tradition advanced into the twentieth century. King Chulalongkorn, Rama V, started construction of "The Marble Temple" in 1899. It was completed ten years later. The king's half-brother was the architect and his liberties with traditional style included the use of Carrara marble and curved, yellow Chinese roof tiles, and an enclosed courtyard with 51 Buddha images of various styles. Near the rear entrance is a 70-year-old bodhi tree descended from the tree that had been transplanted to south Thailand from the Buddha's birthplace in India. The present king spent his monkhood in the monk's quarters that are separated from the chapels by a canal. The temple is on Si Ayutthaya Road near Rama V Avenue, close to the Chitralada Palace (residence of the present king) and the Dusit Zoo.

▲▲▲**Wat Traimit**—The reason to seek out this otherwise unremarkable wat (sometimes spelled Wat Trimitr) is the brilliant "Golden Buddha" housed within. For near-

ly 200 years, there was little reason to herald this
Sukhothai-period Buddha image. When found, it was
believed to be rather ordinary, covered as it was with
stucco. When it was being moved into a shelter at Wat
Traimit after being soaked in a rainstorm, it was acciden-
tally dropped. The stucco cracked and the pure gold
image was revealed. It stands three meters high and
weighs 5½ tons. The wat is located just east of the intersection of Yaowaraj Road and Charoenkrung Road,
between Bangkok's Chinatown area and the Hua
Lampong Railway Station.

Nightlife
Bangkok is notorious as a wide-open city when it comes
to nightlife, a reputation enhanced by the presence of
more than a quarter million hostesses, escorts, bar girls,
and masseuses. Some say that the sex industry—stemming
from the late 1960s, when Bangkok served as an "R&R"
outpost for U.S. troops during the Vietnam War—is the
largest single component of Thailand's tourist business.
The most intense concentration of nightclubs, "go-go"
bars, gay clubs, and massage parlors is in the **Patpong
District**, along Patpong I, II, and III between Silom and
Suriwongse roads, and along Soi Cowboy, between Soi
21 and 23 off Sukhumvit Road. Barkers on the street, as
well as tuk-tuk and taxi drivers, often hand out small
cards listing the types of attractions, including sex acts,
available in different clubs. If this is your type of scene,
however, remember that tourists are sometimes viewed
as easy marks for hustlers and con artists. And the prosti-
tution industry could be on the decline as AIDS becomes
an ever more pressing problem.

Bangkok offers a wide variety of more conventional
and less risky entertainment for foreign travelers.
Cultural shows, featuring traditional costumes and classical dances, are presented at most of the big hotels, at
the Silom Village Trade Center, and at such restaurants as
Baan Thai, 7 Sukhumvit Soi 32, Ala Norasing, Sukhumvit

Soi 4, and Tump-Nak-Thai, 131 Ratchadaphisek Road.
The dances performed for tourists are often less-precise
excerpts of full-length khon performances, which go on
for many hours. But the spectacle of ornately bejeweled
headdresses, thick facial makeup, elaborate masks, and
extremely stylized movement is nonetheless fascinating.
The graceful arm and hand motions combined with the
often impassive facial expressions have mesmerizing
effects. Once in a while, the Thai Fine Arts Department
stages classical dance performances at the National
Theater near Thamasat University and the National
Museum.

Authentic, traditional Thai music is a relative rarity in
modern Thailand, although stylized versions are presented in shows staged for tourists. Classical instrumentation
includes melodic percussion instruments (xylophones,
metallophones, and tuned gongs), stringed instruments
(two-stringed bowed lutes, three-stringed "spike fiddles,"
and a three-stringed floor zither), wind instruments (bamboo flutes and the double-reed *pi* and *pi chawa*), and
rhythmic percussion instruments (gongs, hand cymbals,
and drums with leather heads). The instruments are used
in different combinations in three basic classical ensem-
bles, the *pi phat*, *mahori*, and *khruang sai*. Primarily a
court phenomenon, **Thai classical music** has declined
in the years in the six decades since the establishment of
a more Western-style government but is preserved in
such institutions as the Department of Fine Arts. Thai folk
music can still be heard in the northern countryside
played primarily on the *khaen*, a mournful sounding
wind instrument made of bound bamboo tubes, each
with a metal resonator inside.

Thai boxing, the acrobatic form of fighting in which
everything goes but head-butting, is the national sport
and a popular tourist attraction. Carried off against the
swelling and ebbing sounds of traditional music, the
fights are like a brutal cross between martial arts and
modern dance. Thai boxing developed from self-defense

into a sport during the Ayutthaya period. It has evolved a complex pattern of rituals surrounding the actual fight—kneeling, bowing, armbands, headbands, amulets. One of its unique aspects is the ongoing musical four-piece orchestral accompaniment that serves as a soundtrack and drives the boxers into greater frenzies. The boxers wear gloves but are allowed to use nearly every part of their bodies. What could spill over into total chaos actually assumes the shape of highly disciplined, intricately timed artistic movement, although the stakes can be high in these prize fights and the boxers (and the audiences) are fiercely intense about the competition. Fights are held at the Lumpini Stadium on Rama IV Road, Tuesday, Friday, and Saturday evenings at 6:00 p.m., with a Saturday matinee at 1:30 p.m. Seats are from 30 to 150 baht ($1.20-$6). At Rajadamnoen Stadium, on Rajadamnern Nok Avenue, matches are held on Monday, Wednesday, and Thursday at 6:00 p.m. and Sunday at 5:00 and 8:00 p.m.; admission is 125 to 550 baht ($5-$22).

Helpful Hint

The Tourist Authority of Thailand, or "T.A.T.," has its head office at 4 Rajadamnern Nok Avenue, not far from the Democracy Monument, tel. 282-1143. The friendly staff can answer questions, provide maps, pamphlets, brochures, bus and train schedules, and reams of other helpful information about Bangkok and the rest of Thailand.

BANGKOK WATERWAYS

Next to the tranquility offered by the courtyards and chapels of Bangkok's temples, the most peaceful respite from the city's wild disorder is on its many waterways. Before the building booms of the twentieth century, the canals, or klongs, were such an important part of Bangkok's transportation system that the city was known as the Venice of the East. Today you will witness life on the water, Thai style, visit the most venerated spot where Buddhism was introduced into what is now Thailand, and stop at the infamous Bridge on the River Kwai.

Suggested Schedule	
5:00 a.m.	Rise for early breakfast.
6:00 a.m.	Depart for all-day trip to the Floating Market at Damnoen Saduak, Nakhon Pathom, and River Kwai.
4:00 p.m.	Relax at hotel.
7:00 p.m.	Dinner.

Getting Around
Nearly every tourist hotel in Bangkok has a tour information desk or a tour program of its own which includes trips to the Floating Market and Nakhon Pathom. Book your trip one or two days before you plan to go. You can also guide yourself. Public buses leave Bangkok's Southern Terminal for Nakhon Pathom every 20 minutes from 6:00 a.m. The trip costs 13 baht ($0.52) and takes one hour, then you can switch for the 40-minute ride to Damnoen Saduak. Direct buses to Damnoen Saduak depart Bangkok's Southern Terminal every 20 minutes, starting at 6:00 a.m. The trip takes 2 hours and costs 60 baht ($2.40). Water taxis take you through the canal.

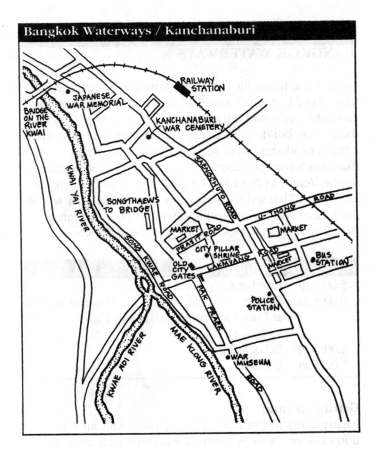

Bangkok Waterways / Kanchanaburi

Sightseeing Highlights

▲▲▲**Floating Market**—The floating market closest to Bangkok proper, at Thonburi on Klong Dao Kanong, is one of Bangkok's most commercially exploited attractions. So even the Tourist Authority has been sending tourists southwest to the less overrun water market at Damnoen Saduak in Ratchaburi Province. Famous for its selections of native fruits and vegetables, this floating market is less tainted by tourism but is rapidly becoming a popular addition to package tours.

Floating markets enjoy a long and important tradition in Thailand. At the crack of dawn, people would congregate on the waterways to buy, sell, and barter for fresh produce brought by boat from the surrounding farmlands. Today, the commerce includes all kinds of souvenir items as well. From their long wooden boats, women sell their bananas, coconut milk, straw hats, and other items to tourists. But if you arrive early at Damnoen Saduak, you will get a colorful glimpse of a sort of bustling trade that is still exotic to Westerners. And you will be able to sample such delicious indigenous fruits as sam-o, the large pomelo that resembles a grapefruit. Along the main canal you will find the Talaat Ton Khem and Talaat Hia Kui Tow markets. The Talaat Khun Phitak market is a short water ride south.

▲▲▲**Phra Pathom Chedi**—The town of Nakhon Pathom, 54 km west of Bangkok, is best known for this towering chedi. The dome-shaped pagoda, crowned with a steep spire, stands 127 meters high and overwhelms all of its surroundings. The original chedi was built during the Mon Empire in the sixth century but was ruined during the Burmese invasion of 1057. In the mid-nineteenth century, King Mongkut, realizing the historical significance of the Buddhist monument—the oldest in Thailand—initiated a plan to make it the biggest as well. After failed attempts at repair and construction over the original chedi under Mongkut, King Chulalongkorn supervised the completion of the present structure. Set in a large square park atop a circular terrace, the bell-shaped dome is clad in orange tiles from China, and its contours are accented at night by glimmering necklaces of lights. A celebratory fair is held on the temple grounds for three days every November. A small museum is open Wednesday through Sunday.

▲▲**Sanam Chand Palace**—Located on the west side of Nakhon Pathom town, this former palace (now government offices) was built as a summer residence by King Rama VI when canal travel to Nakhon Pathom was popular. The king's favorite dog, Yaleh, allegedly so fierce that it was poisoned by fearful attendants, is immortalized in

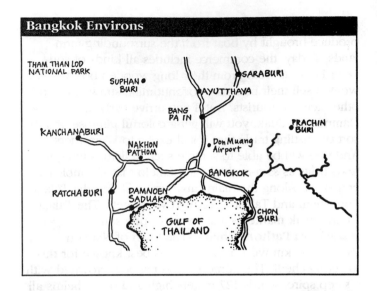

Bangkok Environs

THAM THAN LOD
NATIONAL PARK

SUPHAN
BURI

SARABURI

AYUTTHAYA

BANG
PA IN

KANCHANABURI

PRACHIN
BURI

NAKHON
PATHOM

Don Muang
Airport

BANGKOK

RATCHABURI

DAMNOEN
SADUAK

CHON
BURI

GULF OF
THAILAND

a statue at the entrance. The building, a strange blend of
Thai style and English Tudor influences, is closed to the
public, but the surrounding park, which includes a fine,
renovated *sala* (meeting pavilion), is lovely for walking.
▲▲**Bridge on the River Kwai**—The beautiful landscape
of the Kanchanaburi region, forested hills rolling up to
the jagged mountains along the Burmese border, was the
site of one of the more notorious of many brutal World
War II episodes in Southeast Asia. Kanchanaburi town is
strategically situated for trade at the juncture of the Kwai
Yai and Kwai Noi rivers where they feed into the Mae
Klong. When the Japanese occupied Thailand during the
war, they sought to build a railway to Burma through the
Three Pagodas Pass at the border. Well over 100,000
laborers were forced to work on the project, including
thousands of Allied prisoners of war. An estimated 65,000
died, whether from disease or mistreatment, during construction, giving the train line its historical nickname of
the "Death Railway." Perhaps as many as 150,000 forced
laborers died in the area during the occupation. The infamous Bridge on the River Kwai was a crucial part of the

line. During the war it was bombed several times, including air strikes by the British near the end of hostilities. Several of the destroyed spans were rebuilt by the Japanese as partial reparation after the war. (The original spans are curved, the center replacements have straight beams.) The bridge, which was the subject of Pierre Boulle's war novel and the subsequent popular movie, is situated on the Kwai Yai, 5 km north of the center of Kanchanaburi. During the first week of each December, an elaborate light and sound show at the bridge commemorates the Allied forces' 1945 assault on the Death Railway.

▲▲**Jeath War Museum**—Those who are curious about POW conditions during construction of the Death Railway can visit this unusual museum at the southern end of Kanchanaburi town off Pak Praek Road, next to Wat Chaichumphon. The museum itself is a replica of the bamboo huts that were used by Allied prisoners, with tools, clothing, drawings, maps, weapons, and photographs exhibited to recreate the feeling of wartime conditions. The name Jeath is an acronym derived from the six countries whose soldiers met at the Death Railway: Japan, England, Australia and America, Thailand, and Holland. Admission is 20 baht ($0.80).

▲**War Cemeteries**—Two major cemeteries in Kanchanaburi are the final resting places for nearly 10,000 of the Allied prisoners who died in captivity during World War II. The Kanchanaburi War Cemetery is on Saengchuto Road, north of the town's center, and contains the graves of 6,982 POWs. The smaller and less frequented Chung Kai Cemetery is southwest of town, down the Kwai Noi River on the site of one of the original prisoner camps. Another 1,750 Allied soldiers are buried here.

AYUTTHAYA AND BANG PA-IN

Today, you travel from Thailand's modern capital back in time to the legendary ancient city that was more splendid than the London or Paris of its day. Your tour also takes you to a seventeenth-century royal country retreat updated by subsequent generations of princes and kings. The journey winds down with a luxurious luncheon buffet cruise back along the Chao Phrya River to Bangkok. You sail past the gilded royal barges and the sparkling Wat Arun and observe life along the water against the setting sun.

Suggested Schedule

6:00 a.m.	Rise for early breakfast at your hotel.
7:45 a.m.	Depart for Ayutthaya from Oriental Hotel.
9:30 a.m.	Explore the ruins and wats of Ayutthaya.
11:00 a.m.	Ride by air-conditioned bus to Bang Pa-In.
11:30 a.m.	Tour the summer palace and museum at Bang Pa-In.
12:30 p.m.	Board the *Oriental Queen* for luncheon cruise to Bangkok.
4:00 p.m.	Arrive in Bangkok. Return to hotel.
7:00 p.m.	Dinner. Evening at leisure.

Ayutthaya

An early Khmer trading post conveniently situated at the confluence of three rivers, Ayutthaya was founded in 1350 by Prince U Thong. By digging a canal from the Chao Phrya to the Lop Buri River, the city was made into an island, supposedly impregnable to attack. For the next two centuries, civilization flourished in a Golden Age that was materially represented by thousands of glittering temples, palaces, gilded Buddha images, and kingly collections of white elephants. Foreign traders and diplomats visited from all over Europe and Asia, comparing

Ayutthaya's splendor to that of Venice. But the Ayutthaya dynasty's rivalry with Burmese rulers to the north culminated in the disastrous invasion of 1767, when the great city was sacked and pillaged. Today, Ayutthaya is an ordinary country town, but the ruins of the once-mighty kingdom are fascinating. Some buildings have been reconstructed or restored, but they tend to have less historical resonance than the broken chedis, crumbling foundations, and temple remnants scattered around town.

Getting There

This is one trip worth turning yourself over to the care of an organized tour. The *Oriental Queen* excursion to Ayutthaya is a rewarding splurge. The ticket price of 950 baht ($38) per person includes a surprisingly generous and delicious buffet luncheon aboard the spacious and plush *Oriental Queen* riverboat, plus minibus shuttle service from your lodging to the Oriental Hotel. The three-hour boat cruise is one way, either up or back. The other leg is by air-conditioned coach. The most popular option is to take the bus up to Ayutthaya in the morning and enjoy the leisurely boat ride in the afternoon, arriving in Bangkok at dusk. The problem with returning by bus in the afternoon is getting snagged in Bangkok's bumper-to-bumper commuter traffic. So make your reservations a day or two ahead of time. The tour doesn't allow as much time for sightseeing at Ayutthaya as a self-guided tour—barely enough to take in the most important ruins—but the leisurely river trip is the trade-off. If you'd like to save money and have more time for exploring Ayutthaya, there is regular bus and train service from Bangkok. Buses leave from the Northern Terminal every 30 minutes starting at 5:00 a.m. The 1½-hour trip costs 35 baht ($1.50). Trains depart Hua Lampong station, starting at 4:30 a.m. for 15 baht ($0.60) third class, 31 baht ($1.24) second class, or 60 baht ($2.40) first class. If you opt for a public bus or train ride to Ayutthaya from

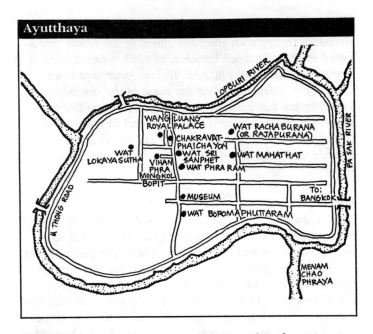

Ayutthaya

Bangkok, you can hire a tuk-tuk or minibus for touring the temples. Prices range from 15 baht ($0.60) for short rides to 300 baht ($12) for all-day tours.

Sightseeing Highlights

▲▲▲**Wat Phra Sri Sanphet**—The royal temple of several Ayutthaya kings originally dominated the grounds surrounding the palace, since destroyed. It once housed a 16-meter-high gold-leafed Buddha image, which was melted down for its 250 kilograms of gold by the Burmese invaders. Now the wat is marked by its three chedis restored in typical Ayutthaya style.

▲▲**Viharn Phra Mongkol Bopit**—This modern-looking building was the result of restoration in the 1950s. It houses one of Thailand's largest bronze Buddha images, the Phra Mongkol Bopit.

▲▲**Wat Phra Ram**—One of the ancient capital's oldest temples, Wat Phra Ram was originally built in 1369 by

King Ramesuan to house the remains of his father, King U Thong, the first monarch of Ayutthaya. It has undergone restoration twice in its long history and is notable for its main *prang*, a tall, fingerlike spire adopted by Thai architects from the Khmer tradition. Wat Phra Ram's prang is richly decorated with images of Buddhas, garudas, and snakes. A climb to the top affords a fine view of the surrounding ruins.

▲▲**Wat Mahathat**—Situated across the lake from Wat Phra Ram, Wat Mahathat doesn't have much remaining after six centuries except for its impressively rebuilt central prang, which at one time housed a revered Buddha relic.

▲▲**Wat Raj Burana**—King Borommaracha II built this large temple in 1424 as the resting place for the remains of his two elder brothers. The twin towering chedis are in better repair than many in Ayutthaya.

▲▲**Wat Yai Chai Mongkol**—Just outside the city to the southeast, this wat was built in 1384 and is marked by the remains of the highest massive chedi in Ayutthaya, a large reclining Buddha near the entrance, and a courtyard filled with 124 small Buddha images. The chedi was constructed to commemorate the 1592 victory of King Naresuan in single-handed combat with the crown prince of Burma—on elephant back.

▲▲**Wat Chao Phanom Choeng**—Also near the southeast corner of town, this notable temple was built some 26 years before the capital itself was founded. The Buddha image in its *viharn* (main temple hall) is the largest one that survived the Burmese invasion, standing 19 meters high. Legend has the image being built in 1324 as penance by an Ayutthaya king who had brought a Chinese emperor's daughter to the capital for marriage. But the young woman grew desperate while waiting for her king to fetch her from the boat and committed suicide.

▲▲▲**Bang Pa-In**—The legends behind this attractive rural retreat are as fascinating as the collection of palaces, pavilions, assembly halls, towers, and memorials scat-

tered around its parklike grounds. King Ekathotsarot of
Ayutthaya was shipwrecked on Bang Pa-In Island in the
early seventeenth century. He allegedly fathered a son by
the woman who befriended him there. The illegitimate
child later usurped the throne and, as King Prasat Thong,
founded a monastery, Wat Chumphon Nikayaram, and
constructed a palace and man-made lake on what had
been his mother's land. The first royal residence was
built in 1632, the year of the birth of King Prasat Thong's
son, the future King Narai. The buildings and grounds
apparently fell into disuse in the eighteenth century but
were revitalized in the late nineteenth and early twentieth centuries under King Chulalongkorn, Rama V. He
oversaw the construction of a resplendent summer
palace, but it was tinged with tragedy in 1881 when a
royal boat capsized and Queen Sunandakumariratana
drowned. A marble obelisk was installed in her memory.
The central attraction open to tourists at Bang Pa-In is
the Phara Thinang Wehat Chamrun, a Chinese-style,
two-story royal mansion built in 1889. But the most
famous building is the Aisawan Tippaya Asna Pavilion, a
delicate landmark of Thai architecture that seems to float
above the glassy surface of the Outer Palace pond.
Around the peaceful grounds you will see a topiary of
trees and hedges trimmed into animal shapes and saffron-robed monks sweeping, strolling, or chatting with
tourists. In late 1989, a new house was being built to
serve as a museum. If you are on your own, you can
reach Bang Pa-In from Ayutthaya by minibus for about
50 baht ($2) or by a 40-minute boat ride for 150 baht
($6).

▲▲The Royal Barges—Housed in a shed on Klong
Bangkok Noi where it feeds into the Chao Phrya upriver
north of Wat Arun, the royal barges are elaborately
carved boats that were used in state ceremonies until
1967. At the end of the rainy season, the king would
bring gifts across the river from the palace to the
Buddhist monks at Wat Arun. The oldest and most

ornate of the barges is Sri Supannahong, a fantastic vessel with tiered umbrellas and an ornate golden pavilion. A crew of 60 was needed to sail it. The barges were last put into action during the 1982 centennial of the Chakri dynasty. The *Oriental Queen* drifts past the sheds, giving you a view of the barges within. You might want to return another time by water taxi to examine them more closely. The sheds are open daily 8:30 a.m. to 4:30 p.m., admission is 15 baht ($0.60).

▲▲▲**Wat Arun**—Located across the Chao Phrya River from Bangkok in the sister city of Thonburi, the Temple of Dawn is one of the most memorable sights in a city of dazzling physical wonders. It is just southwest of Wat Pho and the Grand Palace. In the early nineteenth century, King Rama II decided to expand an earlier temple, Wat Chaeng, originally established by King Taksin as his royal chapel when Thonburi served as the capital. The result of his vision is Wat Arun, with a 86-meter-tall central prang, or spire. Raised on a series of terraces above the soft earth of the riverbank, the spire is embedded with colored Chinese porcelain and shards of crockery that gleam brilliantly in the morning and late afternoon sunlight. The grounds include four small corner prangs, four pavilions housing Buddha images, and many statues. Staircases lead up the tower to a commanding view of the river and the surrounding area. In the misty early morning hours, the beautiful silhouette of the spire earns the temple its name. Water taxis make the short run over to Wat Arun from various piers along the Chao Phrya.

Helpful Hints
Be sure to take your chosen forms of protection from the sun—hat, dark glasses, sunscreen—so that you can enjoy the river cruise without suffering a burn. Binoculars will bring the vegetation, birds, and riverside housing into better view on the cruise.

ITINERARY OPTION: SUKHOTHAI

History buffs who want to delve deeper into the centuries-old Siamese traditions, and wat fanatics who can't get their fill of temple tours, will want to adjust their itinerary for a detour to Sukhothai. The history of Thailand, known as Siam until 1939, is the story of independent Asian civilizations—ancient cultures of the Chao Phrya River basin, the southern peninsula, and the northern mountains—gradually merging into a unified society. The greatest of all early kingdoms was that of Sukhothai. During its century-long reign, Thais were first united under one monarch and a single religion. The ancient capital, some 400 km north of Bangkok, is recognized as the birthplace of the Thai nation. The migrations of peoples through Burma and Laos into what is now known as Thailand gave rise to successions of kingdoms throughout the region. Sukhothai's founding is attributed to the heroic Phra Ruang, whose popular legend includes stories of inventive genius, wily disguises, and supernatural powers, all leading to his assumption of the Sukhothai throne around 1238, under the title Sri Indraditya. Prior to his reign, the people of the central plain were subject to the rule of the Khmer kingdoms centered in Angkor.

It was Sri Indraditya's second son, however, who most shaped the "golden age" of Sukhothai and gave reason for the period to be known as the "dawn of happiness." At age 19, the young prince helped defend his father's state by defeating the enemy leader in hand-to-hand combat. Henceforth he was known as Phra Ramkamhaeng, or "Rama the Brave." He ascended to the throne in 1278 and during his 40-year reign transformed the small city kingdom into a glorious empire. Ramkamhaeng made his mark as an administrator, diplomat, and cultural and religious leader. Under his guidance, Sukhothai became an ally with the Chinese court against the Khmers, a source of innovation in architectural design, a center of production for the Chinese-derived

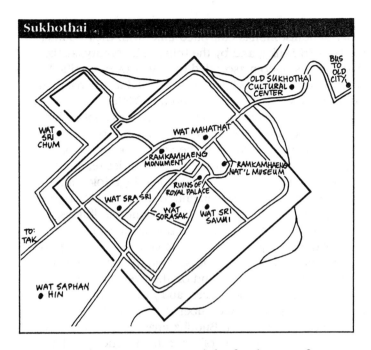

Sukhothai

Sawankhalok ceramic ware, and the focal point of Buddhist religious development with the introduction of Theravada traditions from Sri Lanka.

Buddhism originated in northern India after Prince Siddhartha Gautama, born around 500 B.C., gave up his privileged status and wandered the countryside in an ascetic life-style of fasting and meditation. He attained enlightenment underneath a bodhi tree and his teachings became the core of a spiritual community that spread throughout India for the next five centuries. This early form of Buddhism, called Hinayana (or "Lesser Vehicle"; Theravada in Thailand) became the dominant school of thought in Sri Lanka, while Mahayana (or "Greater Vehicle") Buddhism eventually took hold in China, central Asia, and Japan. Buddhism found its way to Thailand in the seventh century, before the development of the competing schools, allegedly transmitted by two missionaries sent by the Indian emperor Ashoka. Eventually, Thai Buddhist monks cultivated links with their counterparts in Sri Lanka, and by the thirteenth century, as the Sukhothai kingdom ascended to power over a unified state, Theravada Buddhism was adopted as the national religion. Worship centers around the Triple Gem: Buddha; the *darma*, the universal truths as spoken by the Buddha; and the *sangha*, the religious community, specifically the monkhood. The goal is the cessation of suffering, the ultimate cause of which is desire, and to that end, the faithful follow the Noble Eightfold Path of right understanding, right intention, right speech, right action, right livelihood, right effort, right mindfulness, and right concentration. Today, Buddhism still commands the devotion of over 95 percent of the Thai population, evidenced on a grand scale in the ubiquitous temples and Buddha images and on the everyday level of *phra phum*, amulet necklaces, and *puang-ma-lai*, fragrant garlands of jasmine, tuber roses, and orchids that can be seen hanging on Buddha images, spirit houses, and the rearview mirrors of taxi cabs. Practice involves various forms of "merit making," including the giving of food alms to the monks and compassionate and tolerant behavior toward others.

The most important secular contribution credited to King Ramkamhaeng was the invention of the Thai alphabet and script. He employed it in a famous inscription of 1292 in which he described the glory of Sukhothai under his domain. It read in part: "This Muang Sukhothai is good. In the water there are fish, in the field there is rice. The ruler does not levy a tax on the people who travel along the road together, leading their oxen on the way to trade and riding their horses on the way to sell. Whoever wants to trade in elephants, so trades. Whoever wants to trade in horses, so trades. Whoever wants to trade in gold, so trades."

Under the rule of Ramkamhaeng's son, Lo Thai, the power of Sukhothai began its decline even as the monastic influence of Buddhism grew ever greater. The next heir to the throne, Li Thai, ruled explicitly according to the Ten Precepts of Buddha. But military might had become concentrated in the state of Ayutthaya to the south, and by 1365, the balance of power had reversed and Sukhothai was a vassal state. But the first great Thai kingdom left a lasting legacy of architecture and sculpture. One of the most distinctive marks left on Thai style is the Sukhothai Buddha image, characterized by a gracefully shaped, peaceful face and a steeply peaked topknot. The attention to balance and harmony of form carries over into the design of temples, monasteries, and their surrounding grounds.

Today, Sukhothai is a vast park of ancient ruins, partially restored through an ambitious 10-year program. The Sukhothai Historical Park, west of the new town, covers over 70 square kilometers and is dotted with ponds, walls, gates, pillars, frescoes, and Buddha images, surrounded by lovely grassy glades, shrubs, and trees. It takes at least a full day to explore the ruins within and without the walls of the old city.

Getting There

There is no airport in Sukhothai, but Thai Airways has daily flights to nearby Phitsanulok departing Bangkok at 7:10 a.m. and 3:50 p.m. There are additional 10:45 a.m. flights on Monday, Tuesday, Thursday, and Sunday. The flight takes 50 minutes.

Train service from Bangkok to Phitsanulok includes a choice of "Ordinary," "Rapid," or "Express," with three morning departures and five late afternoon, evening, or nighttime departures. The 389-km trip takes six to nine hours and costs 250 baht ($10) for an air-conditioned second-class seat.

If you travel by plane or train, you can make a one-hour bus connection for the 50-km ride to Sukhothai.

Buses leave Bangkok for Sukhothai from the Northern Bus Terminal, with 10 scheduled air-conditioned and reg-

ular coaches every day. Air-conditioned buses depart at
10:40 a.m., 10:20 p.m., and 10:40 p.m. The all-day or
overnight trip costs 190 baht ($7.60).

After your visit to Sukhothai, you can resume the main
itinerary by taking a train or bus to Chiang Rai or by flying to Chiang Mai and catching a connecting flight to
Chiang Rai.

Getting Around

Old Sukhothai is about 20 minutes away from the new
town and can be reached by bus, songthaew, or tuk-tuk.
Many visitors find it pleasant and convenient to rent a
bicycle for the day and pedal around the ruins at their
own pace. Bikes are available just outside the National
Museum for about 25 baht ($1). In hot weather, however,
the exercise can be taxing, especially if you intend to
visit some of the temples outside the walled city. Tuk-tuk
drivers can be hired in town to take you around the ruins
for about 75 baht ($3) per hour. Guided tours can be
arranged through most of the major hotels in New
Sukhothai. The oldest and most informative operation is
in the Chinnawat Hotel.

Food and Lodging

As tourist trips to Sukhothai increase, so do the number
of accommodations and restaurants in New Sukhothai,
the small city that has grown up on the east bank of the
Yom River. Most hotels offer the choice of fan rooms or
air-conditioning. The **Ratchathani Hotel**, at 229
Chodwithithong Road, is one of the newer additions,
with 81 fine, comfortable rooms at 450 to 800 baht ($18-
$32), tel. (055) 661-031. The **Chinnawat**, at 1-2-3 Nikon
Kasem Road, has long been established as a travelers'
favorite because of its friendliness and ready supply of
information as well as motorbikes, minivans, and tour
services to the historical sites. It has 40 rooms (in an old
wing and new one) going for 80 to 200 baht ($3.20-$8)
and a good restaurant, tel. 611-385. The **River View**, at

92/1 Nikon Kasem Road, is another good choice for its location and relatively new, clean rooms, tel. 611-656, as is the renovated **Northern Palace Hotel**, at 43 Singhawat Road, an excellent bargain at 800 baht ($32), tel. 612-038.

Most hotels have their own restaurants and cafés, and the **Ratchathani** features one of the best. The **Chinnawat** is renowned for its bakery as well as original noodle and dumpling dishes. The **Kho Joeng Hong** restaurant, just down the road south of the River View Hotel, serves Chinese dishes, notably stewed chicken or duck in five spices. Try the **Dream Café**, 86 Singhawat Road, for home-style Thai dishes. You can get very inexpensive street fare, including omelets, fresh fish, curries, sweets, and snacks at the **Night Market** next to the bus station.

Sightseeing Highlights

▲▲▲**Ramkamhaeng National Museum**—To acquaint yourself with the layout of the ruins in Old Sukhothai, you can start your tour in this fine museum. It contains a miniature model of the old city that will help you orient yourself before you venture out into the ruins. It also houses valuable artifacts, sculpture, and ceramics that have been recovered over the years. A giant bronze standing Buddha image dominates the entrance hall and is characteristic of the Sukhothai period. There are also Hindu images indicating the persistence of that religious influence during the development of the kingdom. The most valuable exhibit is the famous stone inscription of King Ramkamhaeng of 1292. It was found at the Non Prasat (Palace Mound) in 1833. The museum also sells a helpful guidebook to the ruins. It is open Wednesday through Sunday, 9:00 a.m. to noon and 1:00 to 4:00 p.m. Admission is 10 baht ($0.40).

▲▲▲**Wat Mahathat**—The largest of Sukhothai's many temple and monastery ruins, this important site is presumed to have been founded in the early thirteenth cen-

tury by Ramkamhaeng's father and the first monarch of
Sukhothai dynasty, King Sri Indraditya. The dominant
chedi, shaped in the characteristic lotus bud form of the
period, was remodeled and the tall spire redecorated by
King Lo Thai a century later. Within the remains of the
viharn are giant statues of a standing Buddha and a large
seated Buddha. Nearly 200 chedis dot the grounds in
mazelike patterns within the walls that define the ancient
monastery.

▲▲▲**Wat Sri Sawai**—It is suspected that this temple
predates the dawn of the Sukhothai Kingdom and was
begun as a Hindu shrine to house the image of Shiva.
With the eventual introduction of the monastic Sri Lankan
influence, it was converted to Buddhist worship. Its three
prangs were designed in the Khmer style, with stucco
decorations in the form of fantastic birds and divinities
added in the fifteenth century. The picturesque setting is
enhanced by the still waters of the moat and beautiful
lotus pond.

▲▲▲**Wat Sra Sri**—The close communication between
the Sukhothai kings and the religious masters of Sri
Lanka is reflected in the design of the chedi of this temple. The wat is one of several that had been built on an
island in the middle of a large pond. Six rows of columns
remain from the original viharn, and they define the way
to the central figure, a restored seated Buddha image in
stucco.

▲▲▲**Wat Phra Phai Luang**—Located about 1 km
beyond the northern gate of the walled city, a 10-minute
walk, these extensive ruins date from the late twelfth
century, when Sukhothai was still ruled by the Khmer
Empire. There is speculation that this temple was the
original center of Sukhothai; fragments of stone from a
seated Buddha image have been dated to 1191, during
the reign of the Khmer King Jayavarman VII. Its dominant feature was a central shrine with three prangs and a
brick stupa in pyramidal shape.

▲▲▲**Wat Sri Chum**—The immense, square *mondop*, or shrine, of this temple houses one of the largest seated Buddha images in the kingdom, measuring over 11 meters across the lap. King Ramkamhaeng referred to it in his inscription as Phra Achana, or "The Venerable." Rising to a small space behind the Buddha image's head, a narrow stairway within the enclosure symbolizes the ascent to Buddhahood. The ceiling of this cramped passageway is decorated with engraved slate slabs recounting Buddhist folktales.

▲▲**Wat Chetupon**—Located south of the old walled city, this temple is notable for the mondop that enshrines Buddha images in the four primary postures. Of the standing, sitting, walking, and reclining images, the walking Buddha image is one of the best surviving examples of Sukhothai style. The remaining viharn walls and the wat gates are made from enormous slate slabs.

▲▲**Wat Saphan Hin**—Situated atop a hill about 2 km west of the walled city, this wat is known as the Monastery of the Stone Bridge because of the stairway of giant slate slabs leading up to the temple. The 12.5-meter-high standing Buddha image—another that was specifically described in King Ramkamhaeng's inscription—has its hand raised in the "protective attitude" and contributes to the feeling of serenity that permeates the setting. From the crest of the hill, you are afforded a fine panoramic view of the peaceful plain stretching out below.

▲▲**Si Satchanalai**—A visit to the twin city of the old Sukhothai capital requires adding another day to your schedule. It is located about 55 km north of the old city and was built around the same time as a sister capital for viceroys of the kingdom. The ruins, beautifully situated between hills on one side and a river on the other, are in a much more compact setting than those in Sukhothai. The most important site, attributed to King Ramkamhaeng, is Wat Chang Lom, the "elephant shrine." It has a bell-shaped chedi atop a square base distin-

guished by unique elephant buttresses. Wat Phra Si Rana
Mahathat, about 2 km away from the major ruins, is a
beautiful riverbank temple restored during the Ayutthaya
period with a magnificent prang and a fine stucco relief
of a walking Buddha image. Local buses run from
Sukhothai to Si Satchanalai for a 25 baht ($1) fare.

Helpful Hint
If you've made too many purchases to carry with you on
the rest of your trip, or if you just want to travel lighter,
the domestic terminal of the Bangkok airport provides
luggage storage for 20 baht ($.80) per day. Check your
extra bags or boxes and pick them up when you make
your final return to Bangkok.

ITINERARY OPTION: THE NORTHEAST, NONG KHAI

Until recently, the northeastern territory of Thailand was
almost completely off the tourism circuit. Indeed, as
recently as 1988, one guidebook referred to the region as
"A Problem Area in Transition"—not particularly inviting
but reflecting the history of social and political strife
stemming from the Vietnam War, the nearby internal
struggles in Cambodia, and the continuing plight of political refugees. But during the past few years, both the
Tourism Authority of Thailand and enterprising private
interests have been developing the area's potential for
attracting foreign travelers. Still, the most popular itineraries concentrate on Bangkok, the North, and the
Southern Islands, leaving this vast frontier largely untrav-
eled by Westerners.

Known as Isan, the Northeast is comprised of 17
provinces and takes up nearly one-third of Thailand's
total landmass. It borders Laos in the north and east and
Kampuchea in the south and east, and it derives much of
its culture from Lao and Khmer traditions. This culture,
considered by many to be among the most traditionally

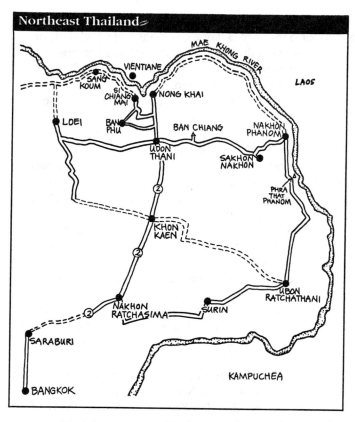

Northeast Thailand

pure in Thailand, is represented in the ancient temples (including some of the oldest Khmer monuments), recent archaeological finds, handicrafts, customs, food, music, and ubiquitous festivals and celebrations. And cultural differences from the rest of Thailand are underscored by Isan's geographic distinctions: semifertile soil that yields such crops as cotton and mulberry trees (which feed the silkworms that yield the raw material for the region's most famous product); fascinating plateaus and rock formations; and beautiful woodlands and forests, mountains, cliffs, and caves, rivers and waterfalls that have inspired the establishment of the Northeast's national parks.

Several provinces and cities have become increasingly popular for one- or two-day excursions from Bangkok or for short stopovers during a spin through the region: Nakhon Ratchasima, also known as Khorat, is both the gateway to and the southwestern transportation hub of Isan, best regarded as a base from which to explore the thousand-year-old ruins at Prasat Hin Phimai and the Khao Yai National Park; Buriram is rich with Angkor monuments and relics; Surin is notable for its annual "Elephant Round-Up" every November; Ubon Ratchathani offers a variety of historic temples reflecting the south-eastern town's situation as a cultural crossroads as well as proximity to the cliff paintings of Pha Taem; Nakhom Phanom is a major spiritual center because of nearby Phra That Phanom, a 1,500-year-old temple ostensibly founded when Buddha's breastbone was brought to the spot; and Loei is revered as one of Thailand's most unspoiled provinces, with a terrain more closely resembling that of the North, a lush, mountainous nation park at Phu Kradung, a forested wildlife reserve at Phu Luang, and a climate that encompasses the greatest extremes in temperature, hot and cold, in the entire country.

But for a short introduction to the Northeast, the province and bordertown of Nong Khai, at the northern frontier with Laos on the Mae Khong River, offer many of the most intriguing (and not incidentally least tourist-oriented) glimpses of the region's history and culture. Indeed, in Bangkok, we bumped into an expatriated American who had resettled in Nong Khai province; he described the area as being "the way Thailand was thirty years ago."

Nong Khai
Situated on the northern border of the Isan region, where the Friendship Highway (Route 2) terminates at the Mae Khong River, the town of Nong Khai is best known as a point of embarkation for excursions in Laos. This small frontier trading center is directly across the river from

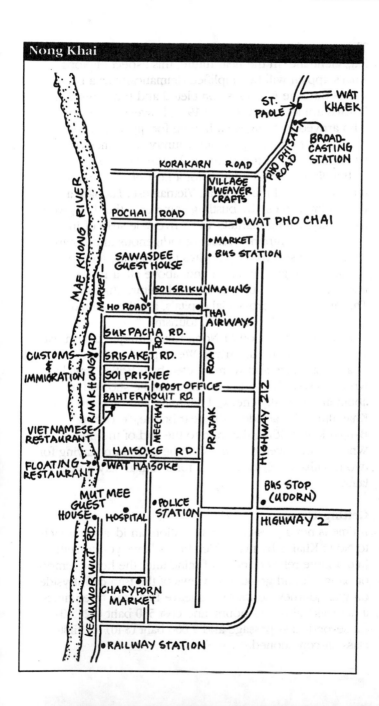

Tha Dua, which is 24 km (15 mi.) east of the Laotian capital, Vientiane. In the near future, this aspect of Nong Khai's appeal will be amplified dramatically as a bridge across the Mae Khong is completed and travel restrictions in Laos are loosened. In late 1991, however, Westerners who arrived in Nong Khai hoping for quick and easy entrance into the neighboring country were met with labyrinthine visa procedures and exorbitant costs.

But Nong Khai is inviting for a host of other reasons: the multicultural mix of Thai, Vietnamese, Laotian, and French influences; the bustling commerce that has given rise to fascinating markets and a riverside strip of intriguing shops; a tempting variety of indigenous and down-to-earth cuisines; proximity to sites of religious, archaeological, and ecological interest; and, above all, a relaxed pace of life and an unspoiled local culture that, in Thailand's larger provincial capitals, are the casualties of "progress," development and tourism.

A perfect indication of Nong Khai's unique charm was revealed to us on our arrival. We stepped into the lobby of a guest house and were greeted by a British traveler who was so at home in the place that he showed us about and virtually checked us in; he had come to Nong Khai almost by accident the year before, "escaping" Bangkok and riding the train to the end of the line. When he discovered Nong Khai, he ended up staying for two months and had returned for a similar stay a year later.

Getting There
If time is not a pressing consideration, an ideal approach to Nong Khai is by rail, which both allows you to settle into a more relaxed frame of mind after the hectic tempo of Bangkok and grants you views of the Isan countryside on your journey north. Trains leave Bangkok three times a day, take about 11 hours, and cost 530 baht ($21.40) for second-class passage and 1,000 baht ($40) for first-class air-conditioned.

For quicker transportation, take a morning flight from Bangkok on Thai Airways to Udon Thani and catch the Thai Airways shuttle from the Udon Thani Airport to any destination in Nong Khai. Flights leave Bangkok's Don Muang domestic terminal at 7:00 a.m. daily (there is also an evening flight on Fridays and Sundays), take one hour, and cost 1,260 baht ($50). The minibus shuttle costs 100 baht ($4).

If you plan to visit Nong Khai before heading to Chiang Mai or Chiang Rai by plane, you will have to plan to leave Nong Khai via Khon Kaen, a sprawling provincial capital 115 km to the south. You can take a morning bus or train from Nong Khai to Khon Kaen and fly to Chiang Mai (on Fridays and Sundays only) at 2:00 p.m. The flight takes one hour and 25 minutes and costs 1,115 baht ($44.60). You can also devise various land and air routes between Nong Khai and Phitsanulok, via Khon Kaen or Loei.

Getting Around

One of the great attractions of Nong Khai is that, as in Krabi in the south and Mae Hong Son in the north, you can see the entire town on foot. It is laid out on an east-west axis on two main roads, Meechai and Prajuk, paralleling the river on the north side of town and Highway 212 on the south. The busiest section of town is on a short loop—Rimkhong Road—off Meechai Road next to the river. For daylong exploring, you can rent bicycles or motorbikes at most guest houses. Tuk-tuks can be hired for jaunts to the nearby wats or to the train station for about 20 to 30 baht ($.80-$1.20); they gather on a corner near the market and the immigration building and you can see the drivers playing checkers with bottle caps on "boards" scratched into the side-walk. For longer forays, there is regular bus service on the highway east to Si Chiangmai, Sankoum, and Chiang Khan.

Food and Lodging

When the bridge to Laos is completed, Nong Khai will undoubtedly witness the mushrooming of tourist-oriented upscale accommodations that will outstrip the current, merely functional hotels. But even then, the homey atmosphere of the local guest houses will be hard to beat. Our favorite in town is the **Sawasdee Guest House**, a modest enterprise in a quiet location near the heart of town. Operated by Mr. Yong, the Sawasdee has a strange, large lobby decorated with wagon wheels and antiques, but the main public space is an interior court-yard with patio furniture where guests gather during meal times and in the late afternoon to share stories and adventures. Except for breakfast, when a gracious helper is on hand to whip up eggs and toast, the small kitchen is run on a communal and honor system basis: you fix your own snacks and drinks and mark them down on your room tab. The rooms are basic but clean and com-fortable, ranging from singles with shared bathroom facil-ities to air-conditioned doubles with hot showers. These latter "expensive" accommodations run 300 baht ($12) per night. Bicycles are available for 30 baht ($1.20) per day. Mr. Yong speaks good English and ensures that the friendly guest house lives up to its posted motto: "You are a member of our family." 402 Meechai Road, tel. (042) 412-502.

The other popular guest house is the **Mut-Mee**, locat-ed on the Mae Khong River at the northwest corner of town. Cottages and bungalows are interspersed in a rangy garden setting, with a common eating area located on the riverbank, with tables and chairs arranged on the sandy ground under a thatched roof. Although geared somewhat more toward backpackers, the Mut-Mee attracts many travelers who appreciate the casual setting. It also has a "travel room" posted with maps, transporta-tion schedules, and sightseeing highlights. Rooms go for 95 to 120 baht ($3.80 to $4.80). Even if you don't stay here, drop by and have breakfast by the river.

For a retreat in the countryside, it's worth venturing east to Thabo, a small town about 25 km from Nong Khai, for the comfortable and attractive accommodations at the **Isan Orchid Guest Lodge**. It is a six-bedroom house with a combination of Thai and Western facilities conceptualized by Don Beckerman, a former New York restaurateur, and managed by Mr. Thom, a world-traveled Thai. Rates are 750 baht ($30) single, 900 baht ($36) double, including breakfast with home baked breads and Isan specialties. The rooms have private baths, hot water, air-conditioning, and fans. Among the pleasures of this rural retreat are the communal atmosphere and the chance to experiment in cooking with produce, herbs, and spices from the market at Thabo, reported to feature the most comprehensive array of wild (nonfarm-cultivated) foods in all of Thailand. The local restaurants are among the most intriguing in Northern Thailand, offering gai yang (roast chicken), som tam (papaya salad), kao neow (sticky rice), and bowls of noodles that call you back every day. The **River Restaurant** boasts an amazing whole duck stuffed with seafood. The Isan Orchid offers a marvelous upcountry retreat—a chance to leisurely explore the unspoiled rural environment or to just kick back, swap stories, and sip a cool drink in the living room. (Although there *is* a "disco" in town, and two funky karaoke bars!) Because of its intimate scale, you should contact the lodge well ahead of your visit; its address is 87/9 Gaowarawud Road, Thabo, Nong Khai 43100, Thailand, tel./fax (042) 431-665.

Eating in Nong Khai is a special adventure. You won't find fancy restaurants (although **The Boat**, the new ice cream shop west of the ferry dock and Immigration Office, is like a spotless Western coffeeshop), but you will find enough choices to keep you hopping and experimenting. Most of the places have names that are untranslated or difficult to spot from the street. Along Rimkhong Road next to the river, there are several restaurants with patio dining overlooking the water. All

offer a wide variety of Thai and Vietnamese dishes at
about 30 baht ($1.20) each. River fish, salads, spring rolls,
soups, and curries are the specialties. For lunch, search
out the small Vietnamese shop three blocks west of the
Immigration Office just off Rimkhong Road, one door
down on the right-hand side of Bahterngjit Road. The
specialties are barbecued pork chunks that you remove
from skewers and wrap in fresh lettuce leaves with noodles, rice wrapper, and fresh herbs and spices and then
dip into your choice of sauces. Two people can have full
orders, plus fried or fresh spring rolls (the best in town)
for a total of 90 baht ($3.60)—easily the best deal in
town and one of the most memorable in Thailand.
Among the other treats in Nong Khai is **Espresso
Corner**, a small café on Haisoke Road—across from Wat
Haisoke—offering real rarities for this part of the country:
brewed coffees from Arabica, Laotian, Jamaican,
Columbian, and other beans, as well as espresso, cap-
puccino and other specialties. If you get to one of the
town markets—on Rimkhong Road next to the river or
on Prasai Road off Prajak Road at the bus station—at the
right time in the late morning, for only 10 baht ($.40) you
can buy freshly baked loaves of crunchy-crusted French
bread brought over from Laos. For a sunset dinner cruise
on the Mae Khong, try the **Floating Restaurant** at 5:00
p.m. It's a little funky and the service is a bit haphazard,
but the food—fish curries, chicken and vegetable dishes,
and more—is authentic and quite spicy with no pretense
to elegance. The boat sails east and west along the Mae
Khong, allowing a fine view of both Nong Khai and the
Laotian side of the river at dusk. Two people can cruise
and dine for 250 baht ($10) or less. To find the Floating
Restaurant, walk west to the end of Rimkhong Road past
the Wat Haisoke and the hospital and follow the signs to
the steep stairs that lead down to the dock.

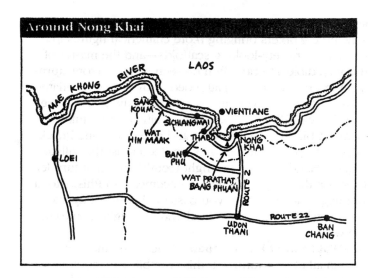

Around Nong Khai

Sightseeing Highlights

▲▲▲Wat Pho Chai—The major Buddha image of Nong Khai province is housed in this recently restored wat at the southeast corner of town. Called Luang Pho Phra Sai, the solid gold image stands 1.5 meters high and was reportedly cast in Lan Chang and brought across the river from Vientiane by General Chakri (who became Rama I). Legend says the boat sank and the Buddha resurfaced on the spot where the wat now stands. The annual Soeng Bung Fai (Rocket Festival) is held here during the full moon in April. To find the wat, walk east on Prajuk Road to Pochai Road and turn right (south).

▲▲▲Wat Khaek—Few sights in all of Thailand exhibit as much whimsical imagination as this fantastic Disneyesque theme park of Buddhist and Hindu images constructed in brick and coated in concrete and plaster. Reflecting the philosophy of an eccentric Brahmin shaman named Luang Pu, this outdoor compound is a garden of outlandish images—a pack of barking and howling dogs, some wearing sunglasses, bearing rifles, or driving cars; towering hooded cobras; Buddhas, Kalis, and mythical hybrids. Construction is ongoing—you can watch the workers bringing more chimerical figures into being from rickety-looking scaffolds—and the master of this incredible site can often be seen giving lessons, turning Tarot cards, or being attended to by young novitiates on a sheltered platform in the middle of the mazelike setting. To reach Wat Khaek, you can either hire a tuk-tuk or rent a bicycle or motorbike and ride east along Prajak Road until you come to Korakarn Road (past the Village Weaver Handicrafts). Turn right (south) and then turn left (east) on the highway where it becomes Pho Phisai Road heading southeast. After you pass the broadcasting station, watch for St. Paole school and turn right (south) to the wat.

▲▲**Wat Prathat Bang Phuan**—One of the most sacred sites in all of the Northeast, this crumbling compound marks the spot where Indian monks were believed to have constructed the original stupa over 2,000 years ago. In 1559, King Jayachetta, from what is now Vientiane, crossed the river and built a taller, Lao-style *chedi* over the first one. It fell over during a rainstorm in 1970 and has been restored by the Fine Arts Department. It is reached by traveling 12 km south of Nong Khai on Route 2 and then turning west on Route 211.

▲▲**Wat Hin Maak Peng**—Founded by an itinerant monk named Thet Lang Si, this monastery is one of the most renowned meditation sites in Thailand, for both the beautiful natural surroundings (bamboo groves in a forest shelter, immense boulders in a towering cliff above the Mae Khong River) and its ascetic monks, whose practices include wearing humble forest-hued robes of discarded cloth and eating only one meal a day. You can get there by taking a bus west from Nong Khai toward Si Chiangmai and Sangkoum on Route 211. From Si Chiangmai, take a songthaew to Wat Hin Maak Peng.

▲▲▲**Village Weaver Handicrafts**—Deservedly the most famous shop in Nong Khai, this enterprise was founded in 1982 by the Good Shepherd Sisters as a self-help project for local weavers. It is operated by Mr. Suan, an English-speaking Thai who has traveled frequently to the United States on behalf of the regional Catholic relief organization that assists with refugee matters. He is a gracious and helpful host, offering refreshing drinks of cold water or hot coffee and tea and dispensing a wealth of information about local customs and sights. The shop sells the hand-woven, indigo-dyed *matmee* (ikat) cotton fabric for which the Northeast is renowned, as well as finely tailored ready-made clothes. The shop/factory is located at 786/1 Prajak Road and can be found by heading east from the center of town on Prajak Road, tel. (042) 411-236.

▲▲▲**Shopping**—Because of its frontier location, Nong Khai is a key trading center and consequently a surprisingly concentrated haven of shopping opportunities. The waterfront market on Rimkhong Road just east of the Immigration Building is the hub of activity where you can find good deals on Laotian silver jewelry and boxes, marcasite bracelets and watches, silver-ball necklaces, woven baskets, silks, Buddha images and amulets, as well as such strange consumer items as VIP Boms Cologne, packaged in grenade-shaped bottles and camouflaged boxes.

▲▲**Ban Chiang and Ban Phu**—If you decide to extend your stay in Nong Khai beyond three or four days, you might want to add day-long excursions into Udon Thani province to the south. Ban Chiang is a small village where archaelogical excavations have unearthed remnants of a culture dating back 5,000 years. There is a National Museum displaying the artifacts of an advanced civilization from 3,600 B.C. and one archaeological pit open to the public. Ban Chiang is located 50 km east of Udon on the Sakon Nakhon highway.

Ban Phu is a district approximately 42 km northwest of Udon noted for unusual geologic formations and prehistoric cave paintings, many of which are within the 1,200-acre park of Wat Phra Buddha Baht Bua Bok, about 12 km outside Ban Phu village. The site attracts religious pilgrims from all over the Northeast and includes a 120-foot-high pagoda and shrine dedicated to the Holy Footprint and Relic of the Buddha. From Nong Khai you can schedule a one-day excursion with one of the local travel services for about 350 baht ($14) per person, including transportation and lunch.

BANGKOK TO CHIANG RAI

Odd-shaped, tree-clad mountains rise from the sloping plains. Rivers and waterfalls course through the jungled terrain. Hill tribes cling to traditional customs just as their tiny villages cling to the hillsides. Today you slip away from the twentieth-century civilization and clamor of Bangkok and land in another world altogether at the heart of the Golden Triangle, where the culture is much closer to nineteenth-century ways of life.

Suggested Schedule

7:00 a.m.	Rise for breakfast at your hotel. Pack for your departure and check out.
10:00 a.m.	Leave for Bangkok airport, domestic terminal.
12:15 p.m.	Take Thai Airways flight direct to Chiang Rai.
1:35 p.m.	Arrive at Chiang Rai airport.
2:15 p.m.	Check into guest house or hotel. Light lunch.
3:30 p.m.	Walk through Chiang Rai and explore the shops.
7:30 p.m.	Dinner. Evening at leisure.

Chiang Rai

Although it is the capital city of the northernmost province of Thailand, Chiang Rai is often dismissed as little more than a backwater jumping-off point for trekkers. But while it certainly hasn't developed into a flourishing tourist center like Chiang Mai, this quiet town has its own special appeal. Chiang Rai Province covers 11,628 square kilometers comprising mostly mountain forests interspersed with fertile valleys. Burma lies to the north, Laos to the east. The city of Chiang Rai sits at an elevation of 580 meters and is bordered at its northern limit by the Mae Kok River.

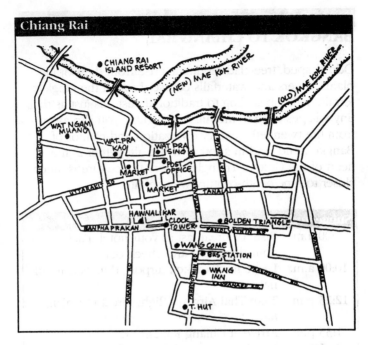

The story of Chiang Rai goes back more than 700 years to King Mengrai, great monarch of the Lanna Thai kingdom. Legend has it that in 1262, Mengrai's favorite elephant ran away and he followed it to the banks of the Mae Kok River. Taking the incident as an auspicious sign, Mengrai expanded his empire and founded Chiang Rai. The region later fell into Burmese hands, was reclaimed for Siam in 1786, and became an official Thai province in 1910. In the 1970s and 1980s, Chiang Rai began competing with Chiang Mai as a center for treks into the nearby villages of such hill tribe peoples as the Akha, Lao, and Karen.

Arrival
Thai Airways offers two direct flights daily between Bangkok and Chiang Rai, departing at 11:15 a.m. or 3:15 p.m. and arriving at 12:40 or 4:40 p.m. The ticket is about

$70. An earlier flight is available to Chiang Mai at 7:30
a.m., with a connection to Chiang Rai at 9:15 a.m. The
flight from Bangkok sweeps over Thailand's vast central
plain and gradually descends over the mountainous
north. The tiny Chiang Rai airport is only a five-minute
drive from town. If you have booked in advance at a
hotel or large guest house, you will be met by a minibus.
Otherwise, plenty of taxi drivers are waiting to take passengers into town for about 60 baht ($2.40).

Sightseeing Highlights

▲▲▲**Silver Birch**—The proprietor of this small shop at
891 Paholyothin Road is a sharp young entrepreneur and
wood carver named Yodchai "Uan" Chalongkitskul, who
studied at the College of Fine Arts in Bangkok. He sells
his own work and pieces by artisans in outlying villages.
The prime attractions are hand-carved ladles, sculpted
from native woods and coconut shell by masters from the
province. Many have intricately meshed moving parts in
the handles. Others take on fantastic shapes from the
plant and animal kingdoms. Some depict graphic scenes
of lovemaking. Be sure to look at Uan's private collection
of masterworks on the wall. He speaks excellent English
and gladly engages in conversation over a cup of freshly
brewed coffee. Since Chiang Rai is a small town, most
artisans and entrepreneurs know one another and can
offer good tips about the latest developments. Tel. 714-
877.

▲▲**Other shops**—Most of the better handicraft shops
are located near the major hotels. **Ego**, across the street
from the Wangcome Hotel, is a large, tasteful emporium
of hill tribe clothing, jewelry, beads, folk art, and
antiques. The selection of silver bracelets, necklaces, and
earrings is especially impressive. Just around the corner
is the **Chaen Saen Shop**, which displays antique
Buddha images, silverwork, necklaces and bracelets, lacquerware, and more contemporary souvenirs in an
almost museum-like setting. The giant **Wangcome**

Department Store nearby sells everything from designer
jeans and perfume to sporting goods, music cassettes,
candy, and dried fish. It's a popular browsing spot in the
late evening. You will also make interesting discoveries
just by strolling around town and poking into intriguing
shops—a music store, for instance, that sells packages of
delicious dried banana chips for 6 baht ($0.24); or a store
near the Clock Tower that specializes in dried or pickled
garlic, dried fruits, and bulk candies, ready for shipping.

Helpful Hint
You can rent small motorbikes at a number of places on
Paholyothin near the Wangcome Hotel for about 300
baht ($12) per day and zip around the entire city on less
than a tank of gas. Remember to drive on the left.

Lodging
In the past few years, Chiang Rai has seen the development of many large hotels that cater to business travelers
and tour groups. New construction continues. The
Wangcome Hotel, for instance, is near the center of
town at 869/90 Pemavipat Road. It is very Westernized
and charges from 1,100 baht ($44) for a basic single to
1,350 baht ($54) for a deluxe twin. Tel. (053) 711-800.
Nearby, at 893 Paholyothin Road, the **Wiang Inn** offers
similar amenities in a slick teak and marble decor. Rates
are 1,100 baht ($44) single, 1,350 baht ($54) twin. Tel.
711-543.
    As Chiang Rai has grown, so have its hotels. The
Dusit Island Resort, on a private island in the Mae Kok
River at the edge of town, literally towers above the competition in terms of luxury—views, deluxe rooms and
suites, tennis courts, a breathtaking swimming pool, a fitness room, restaurants, and so on—at rates of 2,600 to
7,500 baht ($104-$300). The lobby alone is eye-popping.
Part of the deservedly renowned Dusit Thani chain, it is
also Chiang Rai's last high-rise, as a height limit has been

imposed on new construction since its completion. The address is 1129 Kraisorasit Road, tel. 715-777.

There are many reasonably priced guest houses in Chiang Rai—the **Country Guest House, Mae Kok Villa, Chiang Rai, Boon Young**—but the unrivaled accommodation of choice is the **Golden Triangle Inn**, 590 Paholyothin Road, operated by two delightfully friendly and knowledgeable brothers, Junlaphan ("Jun") and Jenwit ("Jane") Sithiwong. It has 39 rooms, 30 in Western, motel-style buildings, nine in older Thai-style triangular hut-shaped rooms around a garden and carp stream. Rates are 550 baht ($22) twin, 650 baht ($26) double including breakfast. The Golden Triangle Inn also offers full breakfasts, lunches, and dinners, domestic airline ticketing, and the invaluable bonus of Jun and Jane's first-name-basis hospitality, as well as that of Jun's popular Pennsylvania-born wife, Becky. Tel. 711-339.

On the river just on the northeastern corner of town, the **Gratom Rim Kok** has been modestly refurbished over the past two years by owner Sumontha Nilkamhaeng, nicknamed Aoy. "Deluxe" rooms (somewhere between guest house and hotel quality), with teak furnishings, air-conditioning, and TV go for 900 baht ($36); economy bungalows, all with hot water and porches looking out on the river, are available at 250 and 300 baht ($10 and $12). Rates include breakfast. The beautiful, spacious grounds have been in Aoy's family for 40 years, and she exhibits genuine pride in her landscaped gardens where many cats (good luck symbols) frolic among the flowers. There's a riverside restaurant and a boat dock for rides along the Mae Kok. 339 Soi Homnuan Paholyothin Road Muang, tel. 716-370-2.

If you really need to get away from it all in luxury, the **Delta Golden Triangle Resort Hotel** (no connection with the Inn) opened in late 1989, literally at the Golden Triangle, just north of Chiang Saen—about 90 minutes by minibus from Chiang Rai. Other than typical resort indul-

gences, there is little to do here but gaze out on the
Mekong River. The food in the spacious dining room is
excellent, serving good river fish curry, pad thai, spicy
eggplant salad, a full Chinese menu, including shark fin
soup and braised sea cucumber, and many other national
and regional dishes. But you will be paying 2,000 baht
($80) single, 2,400 baht ($96) twin, or more for the privilege of staying here. Tel. (053) 777-031. But even this
five-story hotel has been more recently eclipsed by the
Le Meridien Baan Boran, located atop a hill just 2 km
west of the Golden Triangle and designed to integrate its
elite luxury into the indigenous styles and terrain of the
local countryside. Its rates range from 2,000 to 6,000 baht
($80-$240). Tel. (053) 716-678.

Food

If anyone ever suggests that there is little worth checking
out in this quiet provincial capital, just point them to the
T. Hut at 935 Paholyothin Road. Miss Siripan
Boonyarasai, nicknamed "Too," runs this small, elegantly
appointed stucco restaurant, but she credits most of the
recipes to her mother, who helps out in the kitchen. Two
dishes recommended to us by a friend—*nua daed daeo*
(air-dried beef with oyster chili sauce) and *kaeng ped ped
yang* (roasted duck curry)—are just the beginning of a
culinary dream-come-true. The *yam ma kua yao* (spicy
salad of grilled eggplant, minced meat, chili, lime, and
egg) is mouthwatering. Another spicy salad, *yam ped
yang*, includes roasted duck, fish sauce, lime, cucumber,
chili, onion, and ground nuts.

Other specialties are the *kai pad med ma muang*
(fried chicken with onion, cashews, and dried chili), *chu
chee kung* (fried shrimp in curry sauce and coconut),
yam moo yaw (Chiang Rai ham seasoned with fish sauce,
lime, chili, and onion), *moo sa dung* (grilled pork topped
with chili and garlic), *gang keow wan pla krai* (river fish
with salted duck egg in green curry), plus rice porridge
and fresh fruit desserts. Irish coffee from the full bar is

served in a glass that has been dipped in chocolate. Dishes average 35 to 55 baht ($1.40-$2.20), and two people can eat very well for 350 baht ($14). T. Hut is open only for dinner. Tel. 712-162.

The **Golden Triangle Inn** also has a fine restaurant and bar. Ask Jane about the special dishes, and he'll direct you to the steaks. This is not what you came to Thailand to eat, you think, but the pepper steak is wonderful—tender and superbly spiced—and like the filets and the tournedos, it costs only 75 baht ($3) at dinner, 10 baht less at lunch. Generous portions of sunshine beef, Laotian drunken noodles, and pork curry northern style can be had for around 40 baht ($1.60) each. The cozy bar features live performances of traditional northern Thai instrumental music on Friday and Saturday nights.

The **Hawnalikar** restaurant, west on Banphaprakan Road past the Clock Tower, serves Japanese and Thai food in a festive orchid garden setting, with a thatched roof and a running stream full of big, colorful carp. It is popular for its convivial atmosphere and good food. Other popular spots include the **Bierstube** on Paholyothin Road, just beyond and opposite the Wiang Inn, and the **Lotus Bakery House**, a good bet for a quick sweet in an air-conditioned coffee shop setting. You can even get pizza and pasta near the main corner where Paholyothin Road turns right (east).

CHIANG RAI

Today, you will have the chance to guide yourself on a relaxed tour of Chiang Rai's important temples and stroll casually through the streets of the town for a closer look at the local handicrafts and delicacies in the shops, markets, and food stalls.

Suggested Schedule

8:00 a.m.	Breakfast at your guest house.
9:00 a.m.	Wat Pra Keo, Wat Prasingh, and Wat Ngam Muang.
12:00 noon	Lunch.
1:30 p.m.	Explore the shops of Chiang Rai or go rafting on the Mae Kok River.
6:30 p.m.	Dinner. Evening at leisure.

Travel Route
Head from your hotel to the Clock Tower, where Paholyothin Road becomes Banphaprakan Road. Turn right (north) on Triratt Road and walk to Ruang Nakorn Road and Wat Pra Keo. To reach Wat Prasingh, walk east on Ruang Nakorn, two short blocks. Walk back west on Ruang Nakorn to Ngam Muang Road and climb the hill to reach Wat Ngam Muang. After lunch, stroll leisurely through the shops on Paholyothin Road and its side streets.

Sightseeing Highlights
▲▲**Wat Pra Keo**—This humble wat is noteworthy because it is believed to have housed the great Emerald Buddha (now ensconced in the Wat Pra Keo on the Grand Palace grounds in Bangkok). The legend is that a lightning bolt struck and cracked open the chedi and revealed the precious image hidden inside. Today, a

beautiful new replica of the Emerald Buddha is on display. It was carved of Canadian jade by a Chinese artisan.

▲▲**Wat Prasingh**—The chedi and viharn of this temple are more impressive but, like Wat Pra Keo, are still more significant for what was once discovered on this site—an important Theravada Buddha image. The structures are estimated to date from the fifteenth century.

▲▲**Wat Ngam Muang**—The bones of King Mengrai, founder of Chiang Rai, are believed to be housed in a small reliquary inside the ancient brick chedi of this hilltop wat, placed there by one of his sons in 1318.

▲▲**River trips**—One of the most adventurous ways to travel to Chiang Rai is by boat or river raft from Tha Thon, a small village on the Mae Kok north of Chiang Mai. Short of that challenge but still rewarding is a two- or three-hour long-tail boat ride up or down the river. It offers not only the exhilaration of speeding along the water but also grants a new perspective on rural life in the north. Some trips will stop at Lahu, Akha, or Lisu villages. Inquire at the Golden Triangle Guest House or at Rim Nam, located near the bridge that runs north across the Mae Kok River.

▲▲**Lilly Park**—To cool off with a relaxing afternoon swim, take a motorbike or samlor to this park at the southeast corner of town where Prasopsuk Road joins the superhighway. For 25 baht ($1), you can swim in a large, clean pool, open daily from 9:00 a.m. to 6:00 p.m.

MAE SAI AND CHIANG SAEN

Today, you will take an excursion through the northern
hill country into the ancient kingdoms of the Lanna Thai.
From Chiang Rai to the famous Golden Triangle where
the Thai, Burmese, and Laotian borders meet on the
Mekong River, the north is a rich and largely unspoiled
region. You explore the fascinating border town of Mae
Sai and visit the thirteenth century capital at Chiang Saen.

Suggested Schedule

6:00 a.m.	Rise for early breakfast.
7:30 a.m.	Leave on driving tour to Mae Sai and Chiang Saen.
4:30 p.m.	Return to Chiang Rai.
7:00 p.m.	Dinner. Evening at leisure.

Getting Around
Although you can rent a car in Chiang Rai and attempt to
negotiate the roads and traffic yourself, you are better off
hiring a driver for a predetermined or personalized tour.
For 1,000 to 1,375 baht per person ($40-$55), most touring companies or private drivers will take you on a day-
long round-trip to Mae Sai, the Golden Triangle, Chiang
Saen, possibly with stops at a hill tribe village, waterfall,
or elephant camp. Public buses, which are comfortable
enough for the two-hour trips, run on regular schedules
north to Mae Sai and west to Chiang Saen. They leave
from the bus terminal at Prasopsuk and Paholyothin
roads (just north of the Wiang Inn), and fares average 15
baht ($0.60) one way.

Sightseeing Highlights
▲▲▲Mae Sai—This small town, located at the Burma
border 68 km north of Chiang Rai, is Thailand's northern-

most point, the apex of the Golden Triangle. The main road runs north through town, right up to the small concrete bridge that crosses the Sai River, which marks the border. Only Burmese and Thai nationals are permitted to cross between Mae Sai and the Burmese village of Tha Khee Lek, but that makes for a great deal of commerce in this frontier outpost. Scores of shops along the road cater to souvenir-hunting tourists, and hill tribe children often come into town in full native costume, selling the opportunity to take their picture. But there are also many interesting specialty shops where you can find decent bargains on sandalwood carvings, gems, Burmese handicrafts, fabrics, and herbs. The jade factory is especially worth a look; the finest pieces are museum quality and priced as such.

▲▲**Wat Phra That Doi**—This hilltop temple affords splendid views of Mae Sai town, the river, and the nearby Burmese countryside. But you have to climb up 207 steps to get there. Look for the beginning of the staircase on the left side of Paholyothin Road near the Top North Hotel.

▲▲**Golden Triangle**—Although there is little more here than a sign indicating the location, several handicrafts and souvenir stands, and a restaurant, the point identified as "The Golden Triangle" is a popular stop on northern tours. The Mekong River reaches out to Burmese and Laotian shores, and long-tail boats will take you for fast, exciting rides up and down the smooth-surfaced water. In the quiet moments of the early morning or late afternoon, when not overcrowded by tourists brought through in caravans of tour buses, the river delta is quite beautiful and the atmosphere very relaxing, making the Golden Triangle a nice place to stop for a cold drink or light meal. Good fresh and spicy fish dishes are available at the small restaurants that overlook the river.

▲▲▲**Chiang Saen**—Downriver from the Golden Triangle, and 37 miles northeast of Chiang Rai, this ancient capital, founded in the thirteenth century, was

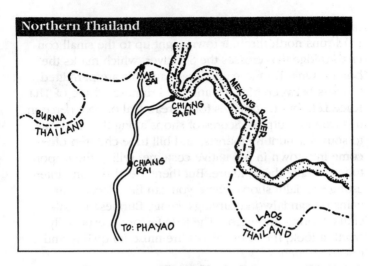

Northern Thailand

the center of power for Mengrai's consolidation of the north. It came under Burmese control in the sixteenth century, was regained by the Chakri dynasty and later destroyed by Rama I, who sought to stave off another Burmese invasion. Rama V initiated the city's resurrection, and in 1957, it became a district seat. Among the intriguing historical sights are Wat Pa Sak, a restored chedi from 1295; Wat Phra That Chom Kitti, a tenth-century hilltop chedi; and Wat Chedi Luang, a thirteenth-century chedi rising 186 feet from an octagonal base. Next door to Wat Chedi Luang is a fascinating little museum with displays of Buddha images and sculptures that have been found among the nearby ruins and intriguing collections of tribal artifacts. Many of the latter have to do with the cultivation, processing, and smoking of opium over the ages. The museum is open Wednesday through Sunday, 9:00 a.m. to noon, 1:00 to 4:00 p.m.

ITINERARY OPTION: TREKKING

Most trek operators offer everything from two-day excursions to six-day treks through the hills around Chiang Mai, Chiang Rai, and the Golden Triangle. These tours typically include bus, car, or truck transportation to a starting point, hiking through the jungle with local guides, travel on elephant-back, and meals and overnight stays with one or more of the hill tribes. To accommodate travelers on tight schedules, some operators have developed one-day "treks" that reveal less of the authentic backcountry way of life but give you a chance to visit hill tribes, ride elephants, or take a raft trip. Your decision on trekking should be governed by your general health, fitness, ability to walk through sometimes rugged and steep terrain in hot weather, and attitude toward visiting indigenous peoples who are essentially on display for Westerners. Your money helps sustain their culture even while increased exposure to the outside world puts new pressures on tribal life and customs.

The Golden Triangle Inn has a tour program with a wide variety of options, from a simple Golden Triangle trip to four-wheel-drive excursions and custom-designed treks to relatively unvisited tribes such as the Yao at Chiang Koeng. The guides, Kamol and Chalor, are Lahu and very familiar with tribal ways. They use no free-lance drivers. In recent years, Jane and Jun have acquired and expanded two houses in Chiang Khong, where their guests can stay overnight on trips to and from the nearby Mon village, rising early for the morning fruit and vegetable market and observing the daylong trade of goods among tribal people.

The best time of year for trekking is the "cool" dry season from October to February. All health precautions, from inoculations to the use of insect repellent, should be taken seriously. Check with your trek operator about what essentials are provided and what items you must bring yourself. (More tips on trekking are provided in

Day 12.) It is also advisable to familiarize yourself with
the customs of the tribal groups you might visit. John R.
Davies and Tommy Wu's *A Trekker's Guide to the
Hilltribes of Northern Thailand* (Salisbury, U.K.:
Footloose) is a good start.

The Hill Tribes

Between 250,000 and 500,000 villagers from various
Southeast Asian ethnic minorities still live in tribal set-
tings, tucked into the folding foothills of the Himalayan
mountain range. There are six major tribes and various
offshoots and subgroups, each with distinctive dress, rituals, and customs.

The largest is the Karen, longtime inhabitants of
Burma, with possible origins in the area between Tibet
and the Gobi Desert over 2,600 years ago. About 300,000
live in Thailand, their villages strung along the Thai-
Burmese border, with the most settlements concentrated
west of Chiang Mai. Many practice an adopted form of
Christianity.

The Meo, also known as the Hmong, migrated from
southern China and number around 70,000 in Thailand.
Their villages, approximately 250, are mostly found near
the Laotian border, north and west of Chiang Mai and
south of Tak. The Meo were among the most prolific
opium poppy growers.

The Akha, originally from Yunnan Province in southern China, migrated via Burma. Their tribe is one of the
smallest and poorest in Thailand. Only about 28,000 live
in the area north of Chiang Mai and Chiang Rai. The
Akha women's costuming is famous for its intricate stitch
and beadwork.

The Lahu, according to some accounts, derive from
Tibetan ancestry and still tend toward nomadic ways.
Other sources place their origin in Yunnan. About 55,000
live in Thailand, largely in tribal settlements near the
Burmese border north of Chiang Rai.

The Lisu are recent twentieth-century immigrants from southern China and eastern Tibet. Legend says they were the only human survivors of a great flood. Only 24,000 in number in Thailand, concentrated north of Chiang Mai and west of Chiang Rai, the Lisu are famed cultivators of opium and practitioners of animist religions.

The Yao (or Mien) migrated from central China during the mid-nineteenth to the early twentieth century. They moved through Laos, Vietnam, and Burma. Most Yao (about 1.3 million) still live in China, another 200,000 in Vietnam, and about 40,000 in Thailand. Their villages are concentrated close to Laos, around Chiang Rai and Nan.

Opium poppies used to be the primary cash crop among the tribes here, hence the name "Golden Triangle." Although the Thai government outlawed and cracked down on cultivation about 20 years ago, when the heroin trade reached crisis proportions and addiction became a national problem, opium-smoking rituals are still part of the guarded indigenous culture. In recent years, development and assistance agencies, such as the royally sponsored Hill Tribe Foundation, have attempted to bring education and health services to the tribes, redirect cultivation away from opium into legal crops, and develop markets for the many tribal handicrafts. Assimilation and "civilization" may be inevitable, but tribal practices and ways of life will no doubt survive for many years to come.

CHIANG RAI TO CHIANG MAI

Today, you arrive in Thailand's second-largest city, Chiang Mai, the "Rose of the North," a busy town brimming with hotels, restaurants, tour companies, and handicraft shops but still retaining a charming, upcountry character. After a casual afternoon exploration, settle back for a traditional Khantoke dinner, then introduce yourself to the bustling and bountiful Night Bazaar, one of Thailand's best.

Suggested Schedule	
8:00 a.m.	Breakfast at hotel and check out.
9:45 a.m.	Ride to Chiang Rai airport for 10:25 flight to Chiang.Mai.
11:15 a.m.	Arrive in Chiang Mai.
12:00 noon	Check into hotel or guest house. Lunch.
2:30 p.m.	Explore Chiang Mai. Reserve dinner.
7:00 p.m.	Lanna Khantoke dinner at Diamond Hotel. Visit Night Bazaar.

Chiang Mai
The Lanna Thai Kingdom of King Mengrai was expanding rapidly in the late thirteenth century when the restless sovereign went looking for a new capital to supplant Chiang Rai. According to legend, in 1296 he came upon an auspicious location where two white sambar deer, two white barking deer, and five white mice were seen together near a sacred bo tree. The resulting town, Chiang Mai ("new town"), developed into the "Rose of the North." Located 450 miles north of Bangkok on the banks of the Ping River, Chiang Mai was the great center of civilization for Mengrai's Lanna Thai, the "land of the rice fields." From the late sixteenth through the late eighteenth century its power declined, only to be reborn in

1796 under the spreading influence of the Siamese Empire. The old part of the city is still surrounded by a 200-year-old moat and fortified gates, while development has expanded the modern city in every direction. As the first center of trekking activity, Chiang Mai has become increasingly popular with travelers, who have sparked a thriving tourist industry. Some visitors complain about the inroads of commercialism, the traffic, and the growing number of Westerners (or *farangs*). Yet Chiang Mai still has a distinctive appeal, and many travelers consider it their favorite city in Thailand. Its people are enterprising and friendly, its spicy northern Thai cuisine is tantalizing, and its art and architecture reflect the diversity of influences—largely Burmese, and to a lesser extent Laotian—that shaped much of the region's history. Chiang Mai is a focus of many religious and cultural festivals, including the Flower Carnival, in February, the water-throwing festival, Songkran, in April, and the candle-floating festival, Yee Peng, on the full-moon day of the twelfth lunar month, usually in November.

Although it is Thailand's second-largest city (pop. 150,000), Chiang Mai is only one-fortieth the size of Bangkok's metropolitan area. Many of its attractive small-town features are intact. Most of the temples, shops, hotels, and restaurants are within an area of less than four square miles, and much of the action takes place in the limited area between the Ping River and the eastern canal of the old city.

Arrival

Thai Airways offers one flight daily from Chiang Rai to Chiang Mai, departing at 10:25 a.m. and arriving 50 minutes later. (A 2:25 p.m. flight is available Monday, Wednesday, and Friday; a 3:05 p.m. flight on Monday, Tuesday, Wednesday, Thursday, and Saturday.) Tickets cost about $17. Thai Airways runs an airport limo service into town for 35 baht ($1.40) per person, dropping you off at any major hotel or guest house. The drive is 15 to

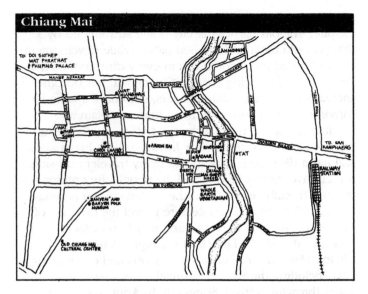

25 minutes, depending on the number of passengers and the route.

Note: You can make free local calls from the telephone in the baggage area. (If you choose to travel by land, air-conditioned buses leave for Chiang Mai every half-hour from the Chiang Rai station. The trip takes three hours and costs 85 baht [$3.40].)

Getting Around
If you choose a hotel or guest house along the Ping River or on nearby Chang Khlan Road, most of central Chiang Mai is readily accessible on foot. Tuk-tuks can be hired, starting at 40 baht, to take you to specific sites or on tours of your own choice. There are also minibuses and taxis for hire all over the city, at negotiable rates: 60 baht ($2.40) for a short trip, 250 to 500 baht ($10-$20) for all-day guided tours. Samlors (bicycle rickshaws) are cheap and fun for short rides but not all that much faster than walking. At the taxi stand on the corner of Tha Phal and Chang Khlan roads, songthaew (small converted truck)

drivers pick up passengers headed for the same destinations. Fixed-route rates are 5 to 15 baht. Four main bus routes crisscross the city and extend into the countryside. The inner-city buses are yellow and the fare is only 2 baht. Bicycle and motorbike rentals are available around most hotels and guest houses. If you choose to extend your stay in Chiang Mai and explore more of the province, countless tour companies and agencies have set up shop in and around nearly every hotel and guest house. **Mai Ping Leisure Tours**, 95/8 Nimmanhemin Road (opposite the Rincome Hotel) is a professional and friendly operation (tel. 215-126). **Bamboo Tour** (tel. 236-501), **S. T. Tours & Travel** (tel. 212-829), **Ping Tour & Travel** (tel. 236-310), **Meo Tour Services** (tel. 235-116), **Chiangmai Honey Tour** (tel. 234-345), and **Lamthong Tour** (tel. 235-440) are just a few more of the many trek and tour services available. With luck and discretion, you might befriend an honest and principled driver who can transport you by tuk-tuk and/or private car during your entire stay.

Lodging

Consistent with its burgeoning tourist trade, Chiang Mai has developed a full range of accommodations, from high-rise hotels like the towering **Empress** and **Mae Ping** to humble guest houses. The **Royal Princess**, at 112 Chang Khlan Road, is recommended if you want pampered luxury in the heart of town. It has 200 rooms (TVs, minibars, etc.), a swimming pool, exercise room, restaurants, and a nightclub, and is located on the street where the Night Bazaar is held. Rates are 2,200 to 11,000 baht ($88-$440), tel. 281-033. The **Chiang Mai Orchid**, at 100-102 Huey Kaew Road, is one of several high-rise deluxe hotels on the outskirts of town. In addition to 267 rooms, it has a pool, restaurants, disco, convention facilities, and a shopping arcade. Rates are 1,452 to 10,890 baht ($58-$435), tel. 222-091.

Probably the best upscale choice away from the
increasing congestion of central Chiang Mai is the **Amari
Rincome Hotel**, beyond the Chiang Mai Orchid on
Huey Kaew Road. Not only are the lobbies, restaurants,
and spacious rooms elegantly and tastefully appointed,
with abundant Thai hospitality at every turn, but this garden resort is neatly situated near a shopping arcade
(Nantawan) and one of our favorite restaurants, Hong
Tauw Inn. It's not cheap, with rooms at 1,900 and 2,100
baht ($76-$84), but if it's deluxe comfort with local
touches you want, you'll feel like your money's well
spent here. Tel. 221-044, 221-130.

Of the midpriced accommodations in Chiang Mai, my
favorite by far is the **River View Lodge** at 25 Charoen
Prathet Road, Soi 2. Neat, beautifully appointed rooms,
with fans or air-conditioning, overlook manicured gardens, a new swimming pool, and the Ping River. It is
conveniently located for easy walks to the Night Bazaar.
The owners, Pitaya Pongpaibul and his wife, Dang, are
very friendly, speak good English, and are able to give
you all sorts of valuable information about Chiang Mai.
They go out of their way to create the most hospitable
surroundings in the city's best small hotel. They also
have a small dock on the river from which they run
evening cruises on their private boat, and you can rent
their canoe for a sunset paddle on the Ping. Rates are
1,000 to 1,200 baht ($40-$48), including full breakfast, tel.
271-109, 271-110. The food is good at the River View's
attractive patio restaurant at riverside, but the proprietors
will graciously recommend their favorite places to eat out
around town. If you can't get in here, try the **Galare
Guest House** next door at 7 Charoen Prathet Road, with
rooms for about 480 baht ($19.20), tel. 273-885.

Within the walls of the old city, you'll find **Gap's
House**, an economical and homey compound of 18
rooms popular with UNESCO and foreign embassy offi-
cials. The singles (only four) at 175 baht ($7), doubles at
350 baht ($14), and suites at 550 baht ($22) are arranged

in a garden setting, furnished with teak antiques, and looked after by Preecha, who has overseen the guest house for the past three years. Although the small dining room serves only breakfast, Preecha often invites guests to join him in a family-style lunch. Bicycles are provided free. 3 Rajadamnern Road, Soi 4, tel. 278-140. The **Chiang Mai Guest House**, 91 Charoen Prathet Road, accommodates travelers on more modest budgets, with 28 rooms, from dorm-style to air-conditioned doubles, at 180 to 420 baht ($7.20-$16.80), tel. 276-501.

Food

The cuisine of northern Thailand, influenced by Burma, has subtle differences in spices (and heat) from southerly regions, although most of its innovations have been adopted in Bangkok. The Chiang Mai specialty is its spicy sausage, available at most food stalls and restaurants. Issan-style grilled, marinated chicken, originating in the northeast, is also popular. The **River View Lodge** serves special northern-style dinners on request, but some of the best (and hottest) northern dishes are prepared at **Aroon Rai**, an unpretentious street-side restaurant at 45 Kotcasan Road.

Our new favorite in Chiang Mai, introduced to us by Pitaya of the River View Lodge, is the **Hong Tauw Inn**, directly across the street from the Rincome Hotel, just off Huey Kaew Road. The proprietor, Mr. Thor, is a gracious host, overseeing a casually elegant dining room with houselike furnishings and a menu that features original combinations such as hearts of coconut with sweet basil and shrimp, deep-fried Chiang Mai sausage, grilled pork salad, catfish curry, and much more, all around 50 to 80 baht ($2-$3.20).

For a beautiful outdoor setting right on the banks of the Ping River, it's hard to beat **Once Upon a Time**, the northern branch of a fine Bangkok restaurant, located a short (but not walking) distance south of the Night Bazaar area at 385/2 Charoen Prathet Road. In this garden compound of teak bungalows, you can choose from a huge selection of such delicious Thai dishes as shrimp with parkia seeds, red curry with beef and potatoes, and winged-bean salad, at prices that reflect the setting—200 to 250 baht ($8-$10) per person for a full meal. The service, by now-solemn, now-giggly waiters, is uneven, however.

Baan Suan "House and Garden," outside of town at 5 Chiang Mai-Sankampaeng Road, Moo 1, is equally elegant and more famous—a traditional teak stilt house in attractive gardens. The **Whole Earth** serves impeccably prepared vegetarian and nonvegetarian dishes, curries, soups, and seafood in a pleasant Thai-style elevated restaurant on Sri Dornchai Road. **Ta-Krite**, 17-19 Samlarn Road, near Wat Phra Singh, is another beautifully built restaurant, with little decks and balconies elevated throughout a garden and lights twinkling on the trees at night. The food is good and not very hot.

No visit would be complete without a **Lanna Khantoke dinner**, in which such dishes as pork curry, sweet and sour sauce (nothing like the Chinese version), fried chicken, fried noodles, pork rinds, and cucumbers are served with both plain steamed rice and the region's famous sticky (glutinous) rice. One of the best combinations of dinner, classical Thai dancing, and traditional music is presented at the **Old Chiang Mai Cultural Center** outside town at 185/3 Wua Lai Road, tel. 235-097. For kow soy noodles, a Thai-Burmese dish of crispy fried noodles in a curry and coconut soup, try **Lahmdoun's**, outside of town, north off Kaed Nawarat Road, opposite Wat Fa Ham. Many different kinds of food are available around the Night Bazaar area, including stewed beef noodles at **Rote Yiam**, Arabic, Indian, and Pakistani food at **Al-Shiraz**, and fresh fish at **Chinatown Seafood**. Chiang Mai is full of smaller restaurants, cafés, and tantalizing food stalls such as those congregated on Loi Kroa Road between Charoen Prathet Road and Chang Klan Road, where you can find crispy barbecued frog skins, fried coconut milk, oyster and mussel omelets, satay, and other treats.

Sightseeing Highlights

▲▲**National Museum**—Located on the northwestern outskirts of town on the superhighway, this small, two-story museum is a good place to familiarize yourself with some of the artifacts of the region's history. The collection of bronze and stucco Buddha images and heads covers a full range of periods and corresponding styles. Impressive exhibits include a huge bronze Buddha head, a Buddha "footprint" inlaid with mother-of-pearl, Samkampaeng pottery, and giant temple drums. The museum is open Wednesday through Sunday, 9:00 a.m. to noon and 1:00 to 4:00 p.m. Admission is 10 baht ($0.40).

▲▲▲**Wat Chet Yot**—In 1477, Tilokaraja, independent king of Chiang Mai, called a great Buddhist council together here to revise the sacred teaching. The temple was built in 1455, copied from one in Pagan, Burma, which itself was a copy of the original Mahabodhi in Bodh Gaya, India, where Buddha attained enlightenment. The name Chet Yot (or Ched Yod, or Jet Yot) refers to the chedi's seven spires, one for each week Buddha spent in Bodh Gaya after achieving enlightenment under the bodhi tree. The square chedi is decorated with delicately carved bas-relief figures, revealing the Indian influence, while the large wooden Buddha inside the prayer hall is much closer to the simplicity of Burmese folk art. The temple is located on the superhighway near the National Museum on the northwestern outskirts of town.

▲▲**DK Books**—There are several good bookstores in Chiang Mai, and DK is one of the largest and best. The vast majority of publications are in Thai, but a big selection of books, magazines, and pamphlets are in English as well. You can find informative guides to Thai history, geography, and customs as well as a variety of maps and many racks of postcards. The store is on Tha Phae Road a few blocks from the Night Bazaar.

▲▲▲**Night Bazaar**—Chiang Mai has plenty of markets: Warorot for dried flowers and clothes, at the corner of

Chang Mai and Wichayanon; Suan Buak Hat for flowers, next to the Suan Prung Gate; and Somphet for fruit, at the northeast corner of the moat. But the Night Bazaar along Chang Khlan Road is the most exciting. Before dusk, hundreds of vendors begin opening up their stalls or setting up on the sidewalks. Hill tribe people come into the city to sell their crafts. By nightfall, the sidewalks are jammed with people and wares. General merchandise stores entice customers with piles of goods and garish displays. There are exotic insects mounted under glass, T-shirts and cotton pants, Burmese beaded tapestries, sizzling barbecued meats on corner grills, and pop music blasting from the tape stores. The street is a peaceful riot of buyers and sellers, natives and tourists, music, food, crafts, and trinkets. The bazaar gets under way around 6:00 p.m.

Helpful Hint

The Tourism Authority of Thailand has a new office in Chiang Mai at 105/1 Chiang Mai-Lamphun Road, on the east side of the Ping River, two blocks south of the Nawarat Bridge. It's open daily 8:30 a.m. to 4:30 p.m., tel. (053) 248-604.

CHIANG MAI CULTURE

This is the day for your closest inspection of Chiang Mai culture, including its historic temples in the old city and its many handicraft workshops on the outskirts. You will also be treated to a panoramic view of the city from the fantastic mountaintop temple on Doi Suthep.

Suggested Schedule

9:00 a.m.	Ascend the mountain to Doi Suthep.
10:30 a.m.	Explore the temples and shops of Chiang Mai.
12:00 noon	Lunch.
1:00 p.m.	Hire a tuk-tuk and tour the silk, lacquerware, silver, umbrella, pottery, and handicrafts workshops on the outskirts of town.
6:00 p.m.	Dinner. Evening at leisure.

Getting Around

The easiest way to tour the temples and handicrafts factories of Chiang Mai is to hire a tuk-tuk driver to take you around for the day. Tuk-tuks won't make it up the hill to Doi Suthep, however, so you will have to ride up on a songthaew or rent a motorbike for the day, which would give you the most flexibility. Start with the trip to Doi Suthep to beat the heat and the bulk of the tourists. Depending on the weather and your stamina, you might choose to walk through the old city, poking around the shops, peering down each narrow *soi* (alley) at your own leisurely pace.

Sightseeing Highlights

▲▲▲**Wat Phrathat**—About 10 miles northwest of town, out Huay Kaeo Road past Chiang Mai University and a strip of luxury hotels, the land begins a steep rise culmi-

nating in a peak over 3,000 feet high, Doi Suthep. Here
sits the dazzling Wat Phrathat, an intricately detailed
mountainside temple rife with gilded Buddha images,
parasols, and gold-tiled chedis. Two long, colorful drag-
ons snake down as railings alongside the 290 steps that
climb to the temple. At the top, you'll find a golden
chedi and intriguing collections of Buddhist relics. You
are asked to wear skirts, sarongs, or long pants inside the
temple. This vantage point offers a grand view of Chiang
Mai and the surrounding hills and plains.

▲▲**Phuping Palace**—Farther up the mountain from Wat
Phrathat sits the summer palace of King Bhumibol, evi-
dence of royalty's good judgment in choosing a retreat
from Bangkok's sweltering heat and pollution. Audience
halls, official buildings, guest houses, kitchens, and dining rooms make up the complex, but only the grounds,
bursting with bright tropical flowers, are open to the
public.

▲▲**Tribal Research Center**—Situated on the campus of
Chiang Mai University, 5 km northwest of the city on
Huay Kaeo Road (the same road that leads to Doi
Suthep), the center is a good place to acquaint yourself
with aspects of tribal life in a setting less commercialized
than the typical shop, market, or bazaar. In addition to a
museum full of artifacts from hill tribes all over northern
Thailand, a small library houses an abundance of litera-
ture on the indigenous peoples. The center is open
Monday through Friday, 8:30 a.m. to 4:30 p.m.

▲▲▲**Wat Chiang Man**—Chiang Mai's oldest temple, on
Rajaphanikai Road, was built in typical Lanna style with
Laotian influences and was the residence of King
Mengrai while he oversaw the construction of his capital
city in 1296. It houses the revered "Crystal Buddha," or
Phra Setang Khamani, and a bas-relief stone Buddha,
Phra Sila, believed to have come from India after the
eighth century.

▲▲▲**Wat Phra Singh**—This large compound, at the
corner of Singharat and Rajadamoen roads, dates from

the reign of King Pha Yu in 1345 and contains a variety of buildings in various styles. The most important is the small, old chapel in which the Phra Singh Buddha image is enshrined. Legend has the statue originating in Sri Lanka more than 1,500 years ago and coming to Chiang Mai during the Sukhothai period.

▲▲**Wat Chedi Luang**—A violent earthquake that shook Chiang Mai in 1545 brought down much of the giant, 283-foot high pagoda here, and the chedi was never repaired. But its enormous base and partial spire, originally constructed in 1401, are still the most significant structures on this Phra Pokklao Road temple ground. The Emerald Buddha was supposedly enshrined here at one time. The legend of King Mengrai says he died close by when struck by lightning. "The spirit of the city" is allegedly safeguarded by the towering gum tree near the wat's entrance.

▲▲**Handicrafts**—Thanks to the tourist influx, Chiang Mai is home to northern Thailand's largest concentration of cottage industries. The specialties of the Chiang Mai region include silk, made from the cast-off cocoons of mulberry leaf-eating silkworms; lacquerware, in which the thick, dark resin of the "lak" tree is applied in many glistening coats to bamboo or teak boxes and bowls of various shapes; hand-carved teak, which is becoming more scarce and expensive as limits are imposed on the lumbering of the vastly depleted teak forests; silverware, from plated bronze and silver-copper blends for pots and bowls to 100 percent pure silver jewelry; Thai celadon, descended from the ancient Chinese Sawankhalok pottery, typically glazed in browns or greens and decorated with intricate patterns; and parasols, with brightly painted paper stretched over delicate frames cut from single pieces of cane. Commerce has grown so much in recent years that nearly every craft is becoming concentrated in factories with air-conditioned showrooms.

All along the Chiang Mai-Sam Kamphaeng Road, east out of Chiang Mai to Bo Sang (the "umbrella village") and Sam Kamphaeng (the center of silk and cotton weaving), are miles and miles of such workshops and factories. Any tuk-tuk or minibus driver will be delighted to take you to witness the making of lacquerware, wood carvings, silverware and jewelry, celadon pottery, umbrellas, and silk. Drivers should charge no more than 120 baht per person for a full tour of the handicrafts areas, especially because many of them are reaping commissions from the factories for bringing potential customers to the door. Along Highway 108, extending off Wau Lai southeast of the town and past the Old Chiang Mai Cultural Center, you will find antiques, wood-carvings, baskets, rattan, and other crafts at Hang Kong and Ban Thawai.

Of course, many of the same handicraft items are available (at marked-up prices) in town at shops like The Jewel Box, 52-54 Chang Klan Road, near the Night Bazaar. Check out the Burmese beaded tapestries, known as *kalaga*, priced from about 400 baht to more than 15,000 baht ($16-$600), in stalls around the Night Bazaar. The shirt shop of Wisut Manasilp, at 15 Charoen Prathet Road, is also worth a visit just to watch him work with his pen and ink, creating amazingly detailed fantasy and mythological images on white T-shirts, denim jackets, and tennis shoes.

For fascinating insights into Thai culture from the perspective of a transplanted Buddhist westerner, look up Mary Roddy, a retired Chicago school principal, at her jewelry shop, Siam Beau Verre. Mary makes her own glass beads, cultivates connections with high Buddhist monks, and dispenses stories and advice at a dazzling clip. Her shop is at 49/1 Chiang mai-Lamphun Rd. (across the Ping from the River View Lodge), tel. (053) 241-245.

CHIANG MAI TO MAE HONG SON

A short flight in a small jet plane carries you through the clouds above the lush green valleys west of Chiang Mai. The terrain grows more mountainous, the rivers more convoluted as you dip into the backcountry toward the lovely village of Mae Hong Son. Soon after you land, you are swept up in the feeling of being in a frontier outpost.

Suggested Schedule	
8:00 a.m.	Breakfast at your guest house, pack, and check out.
10:30 a.m.	Ride to Chiang Mai airport for 11:35 a.m. flight to Mae Hong Son.
12:30 p.m.	Arrive in Mae Hong Son.
1:00 p.m.	Check into hotel or guest house. Lunch.
2:00 p.m.	Visit the Mae Hong Son's lakeside temples and fitness park. Stroll through town or the countryside. Investigate trekking options.
7:00 p.m.	Dinner. Evening at leisure. Early to bed.

Mae Hong Son
Steep hills and mountains covered with thick green forests, broad rivers snaking silently through lush valleys, images of spiky coconut palms reflected on the glassy surface of flooded rice paddies, silvery wisps of fog clinging to the jungle-clad hills—the terrain and climate of Mae Hong Son are the stuff of idyllic Asian postcards. As travelers look for unspoiled alternatives to Chiang Mai and Chiang Rai, they increasingly turn to Thailand's second-northernmost province in the northwest corner of the country along the Burmese border. It is a paradise for nature lovers who enjoy hiking through virgin jungles, splashing around in waterfalls, spelunking in caves, photographing flowers, or watching birds and butterflies.

The population of the entire province (12,681 sq. km) is only 150,000, about half of which constitutes various ethnic hill tribes. Migrations of Karen, Lisu, Lahu, and Hmong peoples into the area started in the mid-nineteenth century, and the town of Mae Hong Son became a provincial capital in 1893. Although it has definitely been discovered, and each year greater numbers of trekkers use Mae Hong Son as a starting point, the town has something of a frontier feeling. During a recent visit, the biggest excitement was a tiny three-ride carnival that had set up at the edge of town, next to the airstrip. The bright lights glowed for blocks in the thick, dark night air, and families came from miles around on motorbikes to put their kids on the small Ferris wheel and carousel.

Mae Hong Son is still much too remote for tour buses, although the runway now accommodates jet aircraft, and there is a Holiday Inn at the edge of town. For now, the streets are shared by dusty European backpackers, hill tribe farmers, orange-robed monks and novices, tidy local entrepreneurs, and a handful of affluent tourists. Unlike Chiang Mai, activity subsides dramatically in midevening. But it starts again before dawn with a fascinating morning market.

The climate here is relatively "cool" year-round, thanks to the shelter of the mountains and the persistent fogs responsible for Mae Hong Son's nickname as "the misty city." Vegetation blooms all year but really explodes in color during November, when the fifteen-day blossoming of the Bua Tong, a kind of golden sunflower, triggers festivities in the province. If you are traveling between November and February, be sure to pack a sweater and consider bringing your own sleeping bag if planning overnight treks.

Arrival

Thai Airways offers two daily flights from Chiang Mai to Mae Hong Son at 10:10 a.m. and 4:15 p.m. The flight takes 30 minutes and the ticket is about $15. The Mae Hong Son airport is literally at the edge of town. Some trails through Mae Hong Son actually traverse the run-

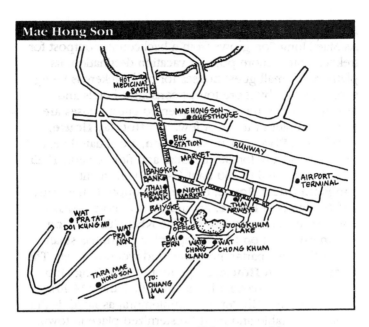

way. Upon your arrival, you will be greeted by representatives of various hotels, resorts, and guest houses, touting their accommodations and offering rides. If you are staying in town and traveling light, you can easily walk the three or four blocks to the center of Mae Hong Son. Note: Buses do run from the Chiang Mai Arcade Terminal to Mae Hong Son for about 175 baht ($7), and the ride through the mountains is stunning; however, the trip takes six to eight hours, depending on the route and the road conditions.

Getting Around
Unless you stay at one of the resorts on the Pai River south of Mae Hong Son proper, everything will be within walking distance of your guest house or hotel. The resorts run regular shuttles to and from town. Motorbikes are ideal for darting into the country or up the mountainside. They can be rented at several places along Khunlumprapas Road, including the Khun Tu Trading Co., for about 150 baht ($6) for a full day, 80 baht ($3.20) half day.

Lodging

As Mae Hong Son grows from a backcountry outpost for trekkers into a more popular vacation destination, its plethora of small guest houses for backpackers is being supplemented by more tourist-conscious hotels and resorts. Many of the most frequented guest houses are near the center of town. A few, like **Holiday House, Rim Nong, Piya**, and **Rose Garden**, are situated near the town's lovely Jongkhum Lake and fitness park. Their rates average 100 to 250 baht ($4-$10) per night. **Jongkam Guest House**, on the lake opposite the wats, and **Sa Ban Nga House**, are among the more pleasant low-budget accommodations. The **Khun Tu Trading Company**, right on Khunlumpraphat Road, has small rooms that are spartan but clean and wood-paneled. The **Penporn Guest House**, at the foot of Doi Kung Moo hill, is another excellent bargain at 360 baht ($14.40).

The **Baiyoke Chalet**, 90 Khunlumprapas Road, is the most comfortable and most Westernized place in town. A standard double room is 800 baht ($32); 1,200 baht ($48) for superior; 1,450 baht ($58) for deluxe. It has a popular dining room and bar as well. Tel. (053) 611-533.

Many people opt to remove themselves from the relative bustle of town (still sleepy compared to Chiang Mai or Chiang Rai) by staying at one of the newer resorts on the banks of the Pai River. The **Mae Hong Son Resort** was the first and consequently it snapped up the best location, right on the banks of the Pai near a tribal village. It is nestled in hills that are shrouded in fog every morning. The mist burns off in the late morning and rises again in the late evening. Cottages, cabins, and huts are scattered around the spacious grounds and range in price from about 875 to 1,100 baht ($35-$44) per night. Room Number One has the best amenities: large double bed, air-conditioning, and a private deck overlooking the river. At first, you might feel isolated from the culture and society you've experienced in towns, but the peace of the countryside takes only an

hour or so to set in. Brightly colored butterflies and
birds flit through the trees, insects hiss in the dense
tropical foliage, and the swift current of the river hums
and gurgles. In late 1989, preparing for the arrival of the
cast and crew of the Mel Gibson feature, *Air America*,
which was filmed largely in the province, the Mae Hong
Son underwent a modest face lift, including the addition
and improvement of bungalows and the construction of
a swimming pool. The resort has a restaurant serving
good Thai and Western food on a patio on the river's
edge, a tour and trekking program, and English-speaking guides. The Mae Hong Son Resort reservation office
is at 50-52 Thapae Road, Chiang Mai, tel. (053) 249-066,
249-391. The local address is 24 Ban Huai Dua, Ampur
Muang, tel. 251-121

The nearby **Rim Nam Klang Doi Resort**, 70/4
Khunlumpraphat Road, is newer and more economical,
with bungalow facilities and 25 tents near the river. Fan
rooms rent for 500 baht ($20) single, 600 baht ($24)
double, and air-conditioned bungalows are slightly
higher. Tents are 175 baht ($7). Tel. 611-142.

As Mae Hong Son experiences the upsurge in
tourism caused by the overflow from Chiang Mai and by
its own natural appeal, it sees the encroachment of
large hotels and luxury accommodations. Fortunately,
the **Tara Mae Hong Son**, a fifteen-minute walk southeast from the heart of town at 149 Moo 8 Tambon Pang
Moo, is a sensible compromise between the imposition
of Western amenities and the preservation of the beautiful environment. A four-star hotel in the Imperial chain,
the Tara has 104 rooms in a block that is wedged neatly
into a woodsy hillside overlooking a swimming pool
and lushly landscaped gardens that slope down to a
creek. The large indoor-outdoor restaurant offers excellent Thai cuisine (as well as Western and continental
dishes), and the locally recruited staff, while still master-
ing English, preserves the regional feeling. Rates start at
1,500 baht ($60) and rise to 3,200 baht ($128) for a suite.

Another recent addition to the accommodation options is the **Mae Hong Son Mountain Inn Hotel**, an intimate lodge with a level of quality and service somewhere between the budget guest houses and the larger hotels. Located just outside of town at 112 Khunlumpraphat Rd., about 100 yards before you get to the much more noticeable Holiday Inn on the same side of the road, it has six twin rooms and six doubles, all with hard beds, hot water, and lots of kitschy Thai decorations. All the rooms face a pleasant garden where guests can gather for breakfast. Local Thais often drop by on weekends to hear traditional music played live in the lovely Thai-style dining room, which looks upon a beautifully landscaped pond and the mountain beyond. Rates are 600 to 800 baht ($24-$32). Tel. (053) 611-309.

Food

Each hotel and resort has its own restaurant, but part of the adventure in smaller Thai outposts is discovering new eating spots around town. You can walk up and down the two main streets, Khunlumpraphat and Panitwattana roads, and sample sausages, fish cakes, and pad thai for as little as 20 baht ($0.80), and inexpensive breakfasts are easy to find. The **Kai Muk Restaurant** boasts an open-air terrace with polished bamboo posts and a thatched roof. It serves a variety of Chinese, Japanese, and Thai dishes, including tempura, spring rolls, ribs, soups, shrimp in chili sauce, chicken with red pepper, basil, and vegetables, frog salad, rice and noodles. The fried cashews with green onion and red chili are delicious with a cold Singha beer in a frosted mug. Prices range from 30 to 90 baht ($1.20-$3.60).

Walk to the north end of Khunlumprapas Road for the bargain restaurants that cater to backpackers and budget travelers: the **Old Home Restaurant** and the **Good Luck** feature vegetarian and international dishes (brown rice, pita bread, yogurt, lasagna, moussaka, tofu) and American breakfasts; **Phue Khun** has cheap breakfasts; I tried the spicy frog with chili at the **Fern Pub** (not to be confused with the Bai-Fern) but did better with the 20 baht ($0.80) pad thai and a large Singha. The cheapest meals can be had at the bustling **Night Market** near the "center" of town. Try the spicy grilled sausages sold at curbside; they're only 4 baht ($0.16).

The **Fern** (or Bai-Fern), across the street and south toward the post office from the Baiyoke Chalet, is Mae Hong Son's upscale restaurant, featuring rattan chairs, dark wood, and soft lights, and decorated with ferns, orchids, and red and pink anthuriums. It is open to the street, with a narrow strip of garden patio seating near the sidewalk. In the evenings, you'll hear Western pop music—John Lennon, Simon and Garfunkel, Sinatra—and jazz on the stereo. The menu is elaborate and rewarding. The pad thai is especially good, and so is the spicy minced fish salad, but you'll probably have a hard time choosing between such delicacies as the fried Pai River fish with garlic and pepper, the various curries, chicken with red pepper and basil, and the coconut milk soup, from a menu with 143 dishes. Dishes cost 30 to 60 baht ($1.20-$1.80). For dessert, the Fern offers a variety of ice cream treats, including such special sundaes as the "Rainbow" and the "Three Camarades" that come out a little different every time, for only 8 to 18 baht ($0.32-$0.72). You'll probably want to make several visits here.

Sightseeing Highlights
▲▲▲**Jongkhum Lake**—The perfect place to wind down after a day of travel and relocation, this pretty little freshwater lake is in the southwest corner of town. An obvious source of civic pride, it has a fitness park around the north side, a miniature playground for children, and benches and pavilions for just resting and contemplating the gorgeous scenery. A large solitary mountain rises up in the east. An ornately trimmed, Burmese-style wat with golden spires casts its reflection on the still surface of the water. Monks walk quietly to and from the lakeside

monastery. Just sit and watch the shadows lengthen and the warm light of sunset cast a magical glow on the peaceful scene.

▲▲▲**Wat Chong Klang and Wat Chong Khum—** These twin temples are located on the southern side of Jongkhum Lake. As fascinating as they are from the outside, they are more important for what they house. The most revered Buddha image in Mae Hong Son, apparently cast in Burma and found in the Pai River, is sheltered here and brought out only for the Songkran Festival Parade every April. There are also brilliant paintings on glass depicting scenes and stories from the life of Buddha, and fascinating hand-carved wooden images of people from various walks of life, all brought from Burma a hundred or so years ago.

▲▲**Other temples around town—**Wat Hua Wiang, next to the site of the morning market on Panitwattana Road, houses an important replica of a revered Burmese image, Phra Chao Pha Ra La Kheng. Wat Klang Tung, near the airport terminal at the end of Sing Hanat Bomrung Road, is interesting for its massive size and modern version of traditional architecture. Wat Don Jedee is another large temple, on the northern edge of town, west off Khunlumpraphat Road next to a hot springs medicinal bath, which might be just what you need after a morning of travel and an afternoon of temple touring.

MAE HONG SON: MORNING MARKET AND TEMPLES

Today, you wander through one of the most absorbing scenes in all of Thailand, the morning market of Mae Hong Son, where farm families bring their produce, fish, and meat to sell at the crack of dawn. Later, you look out over the entire valley from the peaceful surroundings of the "Temple on the Hill." In the afternoon, take a long-tail boat ride up the Pai River or a brief elephant ride through the jungle.

Suggested Schedule

5:00 a.m.	Rise early for the morning market.
8:00 a.m.	Breakfast.
9:30 a.m.	Visit Wat Prathat Doi Khun Mu.
12:00 noon	Lunch.
1:00 p.m.	River trip on the Pai or elephant ride in the jungle.
6:00 p.m.	Dinner. Evening at leisure. Early to bed in preparation for trekking.

Travel Route

To reach the morning market, walk north on Khunlumpraphat Road and turn right (east) on Sing Hanat Bomrung Road. After one block look to your left: the market is set up between Sing Hanat Bomrung and Panitwattana roads. The easiest way to reach Wat Prathat Doi Khun Mu is by motorbike, but you can walk by taking the path that starts on the west side of Khunlumpraphat Road across from the Me Tee Hotel. Stay to your left until you reach the temple entrance. Then continue up the hill on the old stairway or walk along the paved road. The climb takes about half an hour.

Sightseeing Highlights

▲▲▲**Morning Market**—The people of Mae Hong Son
still do their shopping the old-fashioned way: they congregate in an open-air market every morning to buy fresh
fruits, vegetables, flowers, poultry, and fish as well as a
few prepared treats and certain hard goods for the
household. Unlike night markets, which tend toward
more handcrafted and manufactured items, the morning
market is primarily a cornucopia of food. People are setting up even before the sun comes up, and most
Westerners don't show up until the "decent hours" of
seven or eight. By arriving at dawn, you will be part of
the customary scene as it has been taking place for
decades.

Women lay out mats, blankets, and newspapers and
arrange tidy displays of bananas, tomatoes, cabbages,
sugarcane, greens, dried and salted fish, and other food-
stuffs. They dole out red, green, and yellow chili peppers, peanuts, garlics, and herbs in individual portions
and sit cross-legged surrounded by their goods and wait
for customers. "Flower ladies" are arranging stems of
orchids, gladiolas, and other native blossoms. One family
might be selling eels on long bamboo skewers, while
another is barbecuing river fish on small hibachis. Monks
from the Mae Hong Son monasteries pad through the
market, accepting small offerings of food from the vendors. On one table, a woman has a day's catch of fat,
pink-fleshed fish displayed on broad banana leaves.
Nearby, young girls are chopping up pork and handling
large, slippery cubes of liver. In one corner, women are
tending a huge grinder that is squeezing milk out of
coconut meat and yielding piles of flaky, snow-white
coconut. Across the way, an entire family is watching
over tables of smoked sausages, beef kabobs, noodles
and curries, dishing out hot food for hungry shoppers or
wrapping up packages to be taken home. At the northeast corner of the market, a friendly man with a broad,
gleaming smile is rolling and cutting chunks of dough,

tossing them into a giant wok of hot oil, and manipulating them with long chopsticks while they rise and brown. His young female helpers fish them out with long-handled strainers and sell these piping-hot crullers to passersby. You can sit down at one of the small tables and be served a basket of these treats with small cups of freshly brewed strong, sweet coffee for about 10 or 15 baht ($0.40-$0.60). Around the corner, someone's selling delicious fried coconut, while at the other end of the aisle, another woman and her daughter are making crisp, steaming waffles on a pair of irons. Maybe you won't need breakfast later, after all.

▲▲▲**Wat Prathat Doi Khun Mu**—Any evening at dusk, look up the steep mountain behind Mae Hong Son to the west and you'll see the sun set behind two dome-shaped chedis at the top of the hill. As darkness falls, special strings of lights come on and the outlines of the chedis twinkle against the night sky. At the very top is "The Temple of the Hill," built 150 years ago by Phrya Singhanatracha, the first king of the province. The wat is constructed of teak, with ornate carving and the multi-tiered roofs of the Burmese style. It houses several Buddha images and is the site of an important full moon festival in October. The viharn is tended by shyly smiling novice monks from the adjoining monastery. The youngest boys will pose for photographs only to be teased by the others. On the grounds nearby is a beautiful octagonal pavilion with bright red columns and tiled roofs decorated with gold trim. It is situated on the edge of a cliff, overlooking the town and the valley to the east. Young monks in orange robes relaxing on the white benches of the pavilion, framed by the red pillars against the distant misty green landscape, become part of the most tranquil scene imaginable. From the front of the tall, domed chedi, you can survey the entire region: the rice paddies among winding rivers, the fog-crowned mountains, and the town below.

▲▲**Wat Phra Non**—Located at the base of the hill,
down from Wat Prathat Doi Khun Mu, this temple is
guarded by two enormous stone lions at the foot of the
stairway entrance. The most prominent feature is a 12-
meter-long, Burmese-style reclining Buddha image. The
ashes of Mae Hong Son kings are also housed here.

▲▲**Pai River Boat Ride**—Tour guides contract with
local Karen villagers to buzz up the Pai River toward the
Burmese border in a long-tail boat. The boat gets its
name from the long propeller shaft that extends out the
tail from the motor. The river is broad and flat, especially
after the rainy season. The ride is swift and smooth. You
can see all kinds of vegetation and birds along the shore
as you cruise through the hilly jungle. The boat usually
stops at the police outpost a few kilometers short of the
border to check on conditions ahead. You have time to
check out the humble but interesting temple and
monastery here.

▲**Pa Dawn**—One popular outing is a trip up the Pai
River to see the legendary and oft-photographed long-
necked Pa Dawn women. From early childhood, girls of
the tribe are fitted with ringed necklaces. As rings are
added, their necks stretch to extraordinary lengths. But
the tribal elders keep the women under wraps and
parade them out for tourists at a price, usually about 500
baht ($20) per person, turning a cultural peculiarity into a
zoo-like exhibition of questionable moral value.

DAY 12
MAE HONG SON: BACKCOUNTRY TREKKING

Today, you launch your adventure into the real back-country of northern Thailand. Led by native guides familiar with the trails, the people, and the customs of the hills, you drive, ride, and hike into the Thai-Burmese border territory, taking your dinner with a Lihu or Lahu tribe and spending the night in a village hut.

Suggested Schedule

6:00 a.m.	Rise for early breakfast and trek departure.
7:30 a.m.	Leave by truck or minibus with trek group and guides.
9:30 a.m.	Ride elephants through hill country.
12:00 noon	Stop for lunch in tribal village.
1:30 p.m.	Hike deeper into hills, along trails and rivers.
5:00 p.m.	Arrival at hill tribe destination, dinner with villagers.

Trekking

Trekking is usually one of the most memorable experiences for travelers in Thailand. Hiking in to meet and "break bread" with the hill tribe peoples is a relatively recent phenomenon. Thus treks, even simple "overnighters," are anything but luxury affairs. They can be taxing in the heat and trying on the nerves, but they are especially appealing to the intrepid traveler who wants a closer and less mediated contact with an indigenous population that has minimal contact with modern civilization.

Many villages have been visited by Westerners over the past two or three decades, but many have remained untainted by tourism or even undiscovered until today.

This is especially true in the Mae Hong Son area, because most trekking has taken place out of Chiang Mai and Chiang Rai. Big-time tourist operations are unheard of here, and trekking is still supervised by knowledgeable locals. Almost every agency claims to have guides who are fluent in the hill tribe dialects. Take this assertion with a grain of salt. The dialects vary greatly and are difficult to master. But good guides will be sharply attuned to customs, proper etiquette, and taboos among the local hill tribes. Most tour organizers will also advertise newly found tribes, such as the recently discovered Kyah, and exclusive contacts. These boasts are more feasible, especially in Mae Hong Son Province, but again, realize that everyone is conscious of good selling points.

The insensitive exploitation of hill tribes is not beneficial to anyone. For hundreds of years, these people have lived subsistence existences, relying on their own resources for food and daily necessities. The incursion of Westerners throws new variables into the balance. When the exchange economy takes hold, villagers become more aware of trading their goods, their rituals, their hospitality, even their very presence for money. The most-visited tribes may have adopted whole new sets of values that go along with buying and selling. Some may wear Western clothes, barter for consumer items, pose for photographs in exchange for money, or beg. Tour companies who cater to hardy and adventurous trekkers try to avoid these "spoiled" villages, but much of the responsibility to preserve the traditions and dignity of the tribal people is on the trekkers themselves. In exchange for visiting a remote and relatively untainted village, you may forfeit much direct contact with the people, who, although friendly and hospitable, will negotiate with the guide.

Your travel route will be under the control of your trek leader, but you might have some input in advance if you make known your personal interests. Most of the trekking is done in the territory northwest of Mae Hong

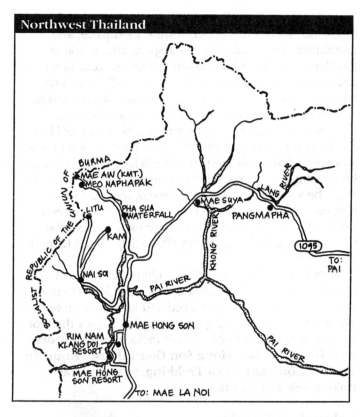

Northwest Thailand

Son, along the Burma border. Typical short treks include motor transportation into the jungle, two or three hours of elephant riding, several hours of hiking, perhaps some river rafting, and the overnight visit with the hill tribe. Longer treks usually involve more walking and stops at several different tribal villages.

Many of your necessities for eating and sleeping will be supplied by your trekking agency. You want to travel as light as possible without leaving behind any essentials. Be sure to inquire about what is provided—backpacks, sleeping bags, blankets? Among the items you might want to pack yourself are bedding (if feasible), a change of clothes, a sunhat, all medicines, sun screens, and repellents, soap, toilet paper, towels, toothpaste, and toothbrush. Leave valuables—passport, airline tickets, traveler's checks, and so on—in the safe of your hotel or guest house (and get a detailed receipt!). Take as little money as possible, under the advisement of your guide.

When selecting your trek, ask every question that crosses your mind. How long will you be walking? How much do you have to carry? Who are your trekking companions? What meals are provided? What terrain will you be crossing? How exposed to foreigners are the hill tribes you'll be visiting? Do the guides speak the local languages? Try to find people in town who have returned from treks and grill them about their experience. Most overnight treks will cost about 300 to 500 baht ($12-$20) per person.

Don Enterprises, at 77/1 Khunlumpraphat Road, is the most established trekking operation in Mae Hong Son. The guides are experienced and knowledgeable. But many operations have sprung up in the past three or four years and are reliable. These include **Lanna Tours, S&N Tours**, the **Mae Hong Son Guest House, Khun Tu Trading Company, Nick Trekking**, as well as the major hotels and resorts.

Sightseeing Highlights
▲▲▲**Lisu Village**—There are relatively few Lisu in the immediate vicinity of Mae Hong Son, but they are among the most interesting for their brightly colored handcrafted clothes (sometimes adopting modern synthetic fabrics into their patterns) and their heavy, ornate silver necklaces, bracelets, rings, buttons, and dangles. They comprise two subgroups, the Ha Lisu (Black) and the more prevalent Hua Lisu (Flowery). Their belief system includes ancestor worship and a host of spirits who may bestow good fortune or bring evil through the possession of human beings. Local shamans provide contact with the spirits and oversee sacrifices. Like the Hmong, they have

long relied on opium cultivation. Important events such as marriage (prearranged through heavy negotiation between the families) and death (believed to be preordained by the god Yelaun) are occasion for elaborate rituals. In the Lisu house, built either on stilts or on the ground, guests usually sleep on a platform in the main living area and should not enter the family bedrooms, touch the family altar, or sleep with their heads toward the fire.

▲▲▲**Lahu Village**—The Lahu people are divided into subgroups with different clothing and customs. The Lahu Na (Black) are predominant, and many have converted to Christianity, but there are also settlements of Lahu Nyi (Red) and Shi (Yellow) along the Burmese border. Black tunics, jackets, skirts, trousers, and tunics are common, with unique subgroup trimmings and decorations. The two-thirds of the Lahu who are not Christian conduct various forms of spirit worship, overseen by the village shaman, who also conducts exorcisms when bad spirits invade human bodies. Red Lahu worship in village temples decorated with yellow and white streamers hung from bamboo poles. Lahu tend to live at high altitudes (better for opium cultivation) in large villages of 15 to 35 households. Health is a major concern, the subject of daily prayers and offerings. Most of the dead are buried in elaborate rituals that prevent the spirit from returning to the village and purify the mourners. Some Lahu use cremation. The houses are typically built on stilts and divided into a living area with a fireplace, a family room with the altar, and a number of small partitioned bedrooms.

MAE HONG SON: BACKCOUNTRY TREKKING

After breakfasting with your host hill tribe, you continue your trek through the backcountry of Mae Hong Son Province, possibly stopping at other villages, rafting the tributaries of the Pai River, and cooling down in the spray of the Pha Sua Waterfall.

Suggested Schedule

6:30 a.m.	Rise early for breakfast in your hill tribe village.
8:30 a.m.	Set out on foot with your guide.
12:00 noon	Stop for lunch with another hill tribe.
1:00 p.m.	Return route to Mae Hong Son.
5:00 p.m.	Arrive back in town. Rest at hotel or guest house.
7:00 p.m.	Dinner. Pack for next day's departure. Early to bed.

Sightseeing Highlights

▲▲▲**Karen Village**—The largest tribal population in Thailand, the Karen have settlements throughout Mae Hong Son Province. They are famous for the colorful weaving and intricate embroidery that goes into their beautiful garments. Their jewelry includes silver and beadwork, and their handicrafts are found in shops throughout northern Thailand. Of the four subgroups, the Sgaw and Pwo are the most prevalent. Some have adopted Christian and Buddhist beliefs, but most worship a chief god, "Lord of the land and water," and make chicken sacrifices at any auspicious occasion—harvest, new year, times of disease or misfortune. A crop goddess is believed to watch over the fields by sitting on the burned stumps of trees around the crops. The Karen nuclear family households are generally clustered around the original village site, and villages tend to be more stable than among other more itinerant tribes. Large gardens and orchards are not uncommon. Livestock often live under the stilted houses. Marriages between villages are encouraged and become the cause for two- and three-day celebrations.

▲▲**Shan and KMT settlements**—Thailand is the site for numerous settlements of exiles from neighboring countries. In the northwest region around Mae Hong Son, there are camps of Shan from Burma and Kuomintang (KMT), formerly of prerevolutionary China. The Shan are the second-largest ethnic group of Burma, and the Shan state is Burma's largest. For the past three decades, Shan have been fighting for their independence and during the struggle have set up camps across the border in Thailand. After the KMT was driven to Formosa, several hundred set up a counterrevolutionary force in Burma, recruiting thousands of hill tribe people in hopes of mounting an attack on China. One of the consequences of Shan and KMT presence in Thailand has been competition between the two over the heroin trade. Both forces have relied on the sale of heroin to raise money for arms. Recent government actions against opium cultivation and heroin production have cut into these practices. Now trek operators regularly bring travelers to visit the Shan and KMT villages. Occasional border skirmishes, however, still limit travel on a daily basis. But news travels fast to Mae Hong Son, and guides are well aware of what is going on in their trekking regions.

ITINERARY OPTIONS

If an overnight trek isn't your style or pleasure, there are many sights around Mae Hong Son that can be taken in on one-day or half-day excursions. You can explore much of the province on motorbike or sign up with one of the small tour agencies for a variety of group or private adventures. The Mae Hong Son Resort, for instance, offers a dozen daily options that can be reserved a day in advance. These include long-tail boat rides up the Pai River to the Burmese border, two- or four-hour elephant rides, trips to the Tham Pla "Fish Cave," the Pha Sua Waterfall, the Nam Hu Hai Chai Hot Springs, fields of Bua Tong blossoms, and different Meo, Shan, Lasu, or Lahu villages. Similar programs are available through many operators in town. Rates range from 300 to 2,500 baht ($12-$100) per person, depending on the number of attractions and the type of vehicle used (air-conditioned vans, four-wheel-drive trucks, etc.).

Sightseeing Highlights
▲**Tham Pla**—About 17 km north of Mae Hong Son on highway 1095 lies the Tham Pla Park. Aside from the lush setting, the attraction here is the large cave whose waters are inhabited by fantastic giant catfish.
▲▲**Meo Naphapak**—About 35 km farther up the road that leads to the Pha Sua Waterfall, just past the old Pang Tong Palace, lies a Meo (Hmong) tribal village, Meo Naphapak. Because it is accessible by jeep, the village is on many tour agencies' routes: the people are accustomed to Western visitors but not as overly visited as many tribes in the Chiang Mai region. The Meo are renowned for their fine embroidery, which graces almost every tribe member's clothing, but especially that of babies. Engraved silver jewelry is another trademark. Villages are typically at upper elevations where opium cultivation was most successful.
▲▲**Mae Aw**—Just a few kilometers beyond the Meo village of Naphapak is a colorful KMT outpost right on the Thai-Myanmar (Burmese) border. One of the last significant KMT settlements, Mae Aw is attracting increasing numbers of visitors, and the villagers here are becoming adept at dealing with foreign travelers. But the often unsettled politics of the region gives the outpost an edge that has not yet been dulled by tourism.

▲▲**Pha Sua Waterfall**—Located in the forest park of the same name, 28 km north of Mae Hong Son, the Pha Sua Waterfall is actually a series of broad cataracts descending seven levels, spraying foam and creating rainbows in the mist. It is one of the most impressive waterfalls in northern Thailand.

DAY 14
MAE HONG SON TO KOH SAMUI

You will spend much of the day in transit, making airline connections to Chiang Mai, Bangkok, and finally Koh Samui. But by late afternoon, you will disembark in yet another world, and by dusk, you will be strolling along one of southern Thailand's many white sand beaches and wading in the warm, gentle waters of the Gulf.

Suggested Schedule

8:30 a.m.	Breakfast at your hotel or guest house.
10:00 a.m.	Ride to airport for 11:10 a.m. flight to Bangkok.
3:00 p.m.	Check in for 4:00 p.m. flight to Koh Samui.
5:00 p.m.	Arrive at Koh Samui.
6:00 p.m.	Check into bungalow. Dinner and evening at leisure.

Travel Route
Thai Airways flies daily between Mae Hong Son and Bangkok. Bangkok Airways now has six to eight flights daily from Bangkok to Koh Samui, but the schedule is subject to change, especially between low and high season.

Koh Samui
Once the province of budget and backpacking travelers, Koh Samui is now a popular alternative to the heavily touristed coastal resorts at Pattaya (the "Thai Riviera") and Phuket (the large west coast island in the Andaman Sea). It is the largest of eighty islands in the western Gulf of Thailand, only four of which are inhabited. The population of 32,000 was originally sustained by fishing and coconut farming, but as with the entire southern region of Thailand, the area is increasingly oriented to tourists

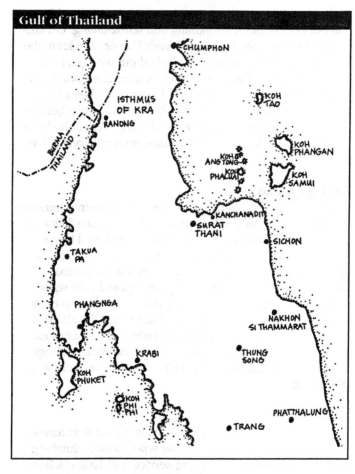

Gulf of Thailand

and travelers from Japan, Malaysia, and the West. A well-paved road runs approximately 34 miles around the circumference of the island, and luxury hotels are now common on Lamai and Chaweng beaches. But low-priced tourist bungalows are still the rule around the island, and it is easy to find an empty expanse of beach. The island interior is 250 square kilometers of largely undeveloped jungle and coconut plantations, criss-crossed by rivers that tumble through the hills and cascade down two major waterfalls.

Coral reefs off the southern and western coasts provide
fine opportunities for snorkeling and scuba diving. On auspicious holidays, such as New Year's Day or Songkran, the
island's buffalo are sometimes decked out with bright rib-
bons and gold leaf in preparation for a uniquely southern
sport—buffalo fighting. The buffalo master recites a blessing and sprinkles holy water on the animals' heads before
they are set loose to engage in the butting battle. The bulls
bash heads and lock horns, wrestling until only one is left
standing.

Getting Around
The Samui Airport is situated on the northeastern peninsula
of the island, between Bophut and Chaweng beaches and
within a 10- to 20-minute ride of most hotels and bungalows. The public vehicles on Koh Samui are songthaews,
small pickup trucks converted into taxis with padded
benches and covered beds. They are marked with signs
declaring their destinations. They charge set rates to each
of the beach areas, from 15 to 30 baht ($0.60-$1.20). You
can rent motorbikes for about 250 baht ($10) or jeeps for
around 950 baht ($38) per day at many hotels and bunga-
lows or in the main town of Na Thon on the western side
of the island.

Lodging
Every kind of accommodation is available on Koh Samui,
from the most minimal bungalow with outside plumbing
to first-class resorts with doting service and lavish buffets.
The best inexpensive to midpriced lodgings are the many
bungalows, ranging from minimal planked huts with
thatched roofs and squat toilets to tidy rooms with fans or
air-conditioning and Western bathrooms. Before choosing
a bungalow, ask about videos: a popular attraction is the
nightly presentation of American films on videotape, usually action or comedy movies, and the sound can get loud
and the audience responses rowdy.

The most beautiful beach on Koh Samui, Chaweng, nat-
urally has the most hotels and bungalows. The **Imperial**

Samui, with more than 70 rooms, lush grounds, and a swimming pool, is one of the island's grand hotels and charges 1,400 to 2,600 baht ($56-$104) per night for the privilege of a visit. The **PanSea** is close competition in the Club Med mold, offering half-board and deluxe bungalows for 1,980 to 2,940 baht ($76-$117). Our favorite accommodations are **The Village**, with fan and air-conditioned rooms at 1,100-1,900 baht ($44-$76), and the **Princess Village** next door, offering traditional Ayutthaya style houses at 1,900 baht ($76). Tel. (077) 422-216.

Prices go down as you move to other beaches. On Lamai Beach, the **Pavilion**, 550 to 1,200 baht ($22-$48), and the **Sand Sea**, 600 baht ($24), are attractive, clean, and comfortable. Bophut Beach is not as pretty as Chaweng or Lamai (the sand is not as white and the waves are not as dramatic), but like nearby Mae Nam, it is less crowded and quieter. Here, **World** offers bungalows that are pleasantly arranged along a garden walk to the beach for 600 to 850 baht ($24-$34). **Sandy Resort** is slightly larger and rents its bungalows for 200 to 1,000 baht ($8-$40). Choeng Mon Beach, tucked into a bay on the northeast tip of the island, offers a restful, private getaway with fine views at the **P. S. Villa** for 50 to 200 baht ($2-$8). Slightly upscale are the **Choeng Mon Palace**, at 500 to 800 baht ($20-$32), and the **Sun Sand Resort**, 950 baht ($38).

Food

Every set of bungalows has its own restaurant, and given the high quality of local cooking, it is virtually impossible to go wrong. The cuisine is generally not as refined or creative as in Bangkok or the north, but it has a refreshing home-cooked character. Seafood, of course, is the main fare, and meals are generally hearty and inexpensive. Two people can eat well on fresh fruit, fish, noodles, a variety of soups, curries, rice dishes, omelets, yogurt, and desserts for less than 250 baht ($10) per day at the midpriced accommodations. Eating where you stay also offers the chance to get to know fellow travelers and meet the locals.

DAY 15
KOH SAMUI: ON THE BEACH

The main reason to come to Koh Samui is to stretch out on the sand, beachcomb, and enjoy the clear, warm ocean waters. Today, you will take advantage of this idyllic opportunity to wind down after two weeks of temple tours and mountain hikes. But you should also spend a few hours taking in some of the man-made sites and natural wonders of the island.

Suggested Schedule

7:00 a.m.	Breakfast at your bungalow.
8:00 a.m.	Set out for exploration of Koh Samui or depart on a daylong excursion through the nearby Ang Thong National Marine Park.
12:00 noon	Lunch.
1:00 p.m.	Continue exploration. Relax, swim, snorkel.
6:00 p.m.	Dinner. Evening at leisure.

Travel Route
From your hotel or bungalow, rent a motorbike or catch a songthaew and ride toward Bophut, turning east at the junction that leads to Big Buddha. From Big Buddha, return to the main road and turn left (south) and drive past Chaweng to Lamai Beach. At the southern tip, turn left where the sign directs you to Hin Ta and the Grandmother and Grandfather Rocks. From Hin Ta, continue on the main road southwest. Turn right (west) at Baan Hua Thonan, where the road heads inland. At about 1½ miles, at Baan Thurian, turn right on the dirt road leading to Namuang Waterfall. From Baan Thurian, turn right, continuing north about 5½ miles to Baan Lip Yai. Turn right to the Hin Lad Waterfall. Back on the main road, turn left (south) and look for the head of the trail to Samui Highland Park. To return to your bungalow, either continue your loop around the island or return back along the same route.

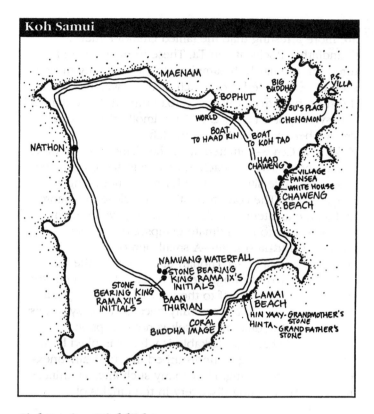

Koh Samui

MAENAM
BIG BUDDHA
P.S. VILLA
BOPHUT
SU'S PLACE
WORLD
CHENGMON
BOAT TO HAAD RIN
BOAT TO KOH TAO
NATHON
HAAD CHAWENG
VILLAGE
PANSEA
WHITE HOUSE
CHAWENG BEACH
NAMUANG WATERFALL
STONE BEARING KING RAMA IX'S INITIALS
STONE BEARING KING RAMA XII'S INITIALS
BAAN THURIAN
LAMAI BEACH
HIN YAAY-GRANDMOTHER'S STONE
HIN TA-GRANDFATHER'S STONE
CORAL BUDDHA IMAGE

Sightseeing Highlights

▲▲▲**Big Buddha**—As you approach Plai Laem Bay at the northeastern tip of Koh Samui, you can see a large figure looming over Farn Isle, as if rising up from the sea. This is Big Buddha, a gigantic seated Buddha image at Hin Ngu Temple and monastery. The massive figure is 15 meters high, dwarfing everything around it, including the other fantastic carved figures of the temple grounds and the nearby row of souvenir and refreshment stands. After walking around the statue, you can browse through the selections of amulets, incense, and jewelry.

▲▲▲**Grandmother and Grandfather Rocks**—The rocky promontories poking out of Thailand's southern waters assume bizarre and mysterious shapes, but none are more arresting than the famed Grandmother and Grandfather Rocks at Hin Ta. These formations are featured on popular Koh Samui postcards, but they must be seen to be believed. You reach them by walking down the short path from the paved road turnoff. "Grandfather" is easy to spot on the right. "Grandmother" is a large crevice between boulders to the left.

▲▲**Coral Cove**—Situated at the headland that separates Lamai and Chaweng beaches, this protected cove is the most accessible site on Samui for good snorkeling and scuba diving. The coral formations are close into shore, so that the amateur free diver need only wade out in shallow water to get intimate glimpses of the reef life.

▲**Coral Buddha Image**—A small sign on the road inland from Baan Hua Thonan directs you to the right, down a dirt road through dense brush. About 200 meters into the jungle, look off to the left and you can spot a decaying statue. Watch carefully because it's easy to miss at first. The Buddha image itself is not exceptionally impressive; what is remarkable is what is implied by its existence. It sits largely undisturbed in a basically unexcavated natural setting. How many such ancient artifacts must still be awaiting discovery in the jungles of Thailand?

▲**Namuang**—Most people never leave the beaches of Koh Samui, so the inland jungles are virtually untouched by civilization. The rivers that flow down from the hills tumble into a large waterfall cascading dramatically down the sheer mountainside at Namuang. At the base is a sandy bottom pool for wading or swimming.

▲▲**Hin Lad and Samui Highlands**—The falls here are less spectacular than Namuang, but the setting is especially peaceful and relaxing. If you are up for a hike, take the well-marked trail to Samui Highland Park. After climbing for about two hours through a rubber plantation and jungle blossoming with wild flowers, you reach the highest accessible point on the island. An enterprising man named Khun Kosol built the park here, with a carefully maintained rock and flower garden. Refreshments are available at the small lodge, and the spectacular views reward your long, hot walk.

▲▲**Ang Thong National Marine Park**—Koh Samui is one of a chain of islands, many of which fall within the boundaries of this national park. Ang Thong means "Golden Basin," appropriate for the entire 250-square-kilometer setting of some 40 protected islands and for the beautiful, coral-laced lagoon where most day excursions stop for snorkeling, although the official explanation of the name is that it derives from the area's function as a major spawning ground for *pla thoo,* or short-bodied mackerel. Most of the islands are lofty limestone formations shrouded with thick, green foliage and jutting out of the quiet sea. The largest are Wua Talap, which has overnight accommodations and is the site of park headquarters; Mae Ko, with one of the finest beaches and a shimmering emerald lake fed with saltwater by an underground tunnel from the sea; and Sam Sao, site of an interesting rock arch formation and a rich coral reef. Passage on the all-day trips through the archipelago can be booked at most of the beach resorts on Samui or through any of the tour operators in Na Thon. The tour includes lunch, snorkeling, and an island stop that provides a panoramic hilltop view of the marine park.

DAY 16
KOH PHANGAN

An exhilarating boat ride across the calm waters of the
Gulf of Thailand takes you one step further from the
pace and pressures of civilization as you explore the next
island out from the mainland, Koh Phangan.

Suggested Schedule	
8:00 a.m.	Breakfast and check out.
10:00 a.m.	Depart by express boat for Koh Phangan from Na Thon, Koh Samui.
10:40 a.m.	Arrive at Thong Sala. Catch songthaew or shuttle boat to beach bungalow.
12:00 noon	Lunch.
1:00 p.m.	Beachcomb, swim, snorkel, or hike.
6:00 p.m.	Dinner. Evening at leisure.

Travel Route
Songserm Travel runs the regularly scheduled express
boats between Koh Samui and Koh Phangan, leaving
from Na Thon Harbor at 10:00 a.m. and 3:00 p.m. The
14-km ride takes 40 minutes, and the fare is 75 baht ($3).
During the high season there is also long-tail boat service
from Bophut Beach to Haad Rin at the southern tip of
Koh Phangan.

Koh Phangan
Despite its proximity to Koh Samui, this island is a
decade behind in development and feels even more
remote than it is. Especially popular among young
European back-packers seeking tropical isolation, Koh
Phangan is nonetheless attracting more mainstream travelers with the same desire to get away from it all. Most of
the bungalows are primitive, bare wooden structures
built on platforms at the beach, most without electricity
or private toilets. They are stretched out along the beach

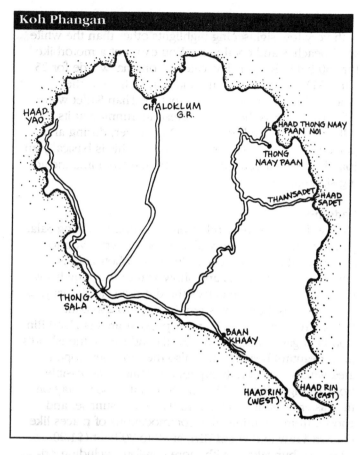

with a centrally located "restaurant"—an open-air, thatched-roof structure with tables and chairs and an adjoining kitchen staffed by a local family. The island's main town is Thong Sala, a village with two main streets of somewhat ramshackle shops, restaurants, and a few bungalows. All roads out through the island lead from Thong Sala—to beach bungalows along the west coast, to Chalok Lum, a fishing village on the north shore, and to Baan Khaay on the southwest shoreline, then northeast across the island to Thaa Paan Bay.

Koh Phangan is a genuine, get-away-from-it-all retreat, with very few sightseeing highlights other than the white sand beaches and coral reefs. You can rent a motorbike for 150 baht ($6) per day, catch a songthaew ride for 25 baht ($1) and check out the interior, or hike to the Phang, Wang Pladuk, Than Prapat, or Than Sadet waterfalls. The latter is the most interesting, running at its fullest from September through November, during and immediately after the rainy season. But this is basically an island on which you can escape from everything, including sightseeing.

Lodging
On the 40-minute boat ride from Na Thon to Thong Sala, young men and women will attempt to recruit you to their bungalows. They carry albums of photographs depicting their facilities and show you to the songthaew that will transport you across the dirt roads to the various beaches. Most bungalows rent from 60 to 250 baht ($2.40-$10) per night. The most popular area is Haad Rin, Koh Phangan's southern peninsula and site of the island's most beautiful beaches. It is also the most developed area with the most fully equipped facilities, accessible from Thong Sala by a 25-baht ($1) shuttle boat. Stay on the eastern side if you want to watch the sunrise, and choose from the minimal accommodations of places like the **Sea View** and **Haad Rin**, at 30 to 70 baht ($1.20-$2.80), or bungalows with more comfort, including private toilets at the **Paradise, Serenity, Chaina Rose**, or **Palita Lodge**, at 80 to 250 baht ($3.20-$10). On the western tip of Haad Rin, the **Lighthouse** offers 15 bungalows, terraced attractively up the hillside with terrific views, for 75 to 250 baht ($3-$10). Farther around to the west, on Rin Nai Beach, where the sunsets are spectacular, you can stay for 30 to 150 baht ($1.20-$6) at any of 16 different operations, the best of which include the **Sunset, Coral, Neptune's, Dolphin**, and **Rin Beach Resort**.

For greater isolation and excellent snorkeling, check out the **bungalows at Haad Yao** on the northern west coast or on Mae Hat Bay at the northern tip. Thaa Paan (or Ta Pan) Bay has two beach areas (Noi and Yai) lovely enough to have attracted King Rama V for royal vacations. You can stay in 30-baht ($1.20) huts or at the 150-baht ($6) **Pan Viman Resort**.

Food

As on Koh Samui, for convenience you will most likely take your meals where you stay, choosing from fresh seafood, spicy chicken-coconut soups, fruit salads, vegetables and noodles, pancakes, porridge, and yogurt. At the budget bungalows, dishes average 25 to 60 baht ($1-$2.40), with prices increasing at the more "expensive" resorts. Places at Haad Rin offer such Western fare as tacos and spaghetti along with the local dishes. Thong Sala has several little bakeries that cook fresh breads, cookies, and coconut treats. One shop owner has big steam pots on the sidewalk outside his store; he dishes out several varieties of delicious Chinese *bow*—soft, dumplinglike buns with savory fillings.

ITINERARY OPTIONS

If Koh Phangan's remoteness and minimal amenities or its increasing population of backpacking travelers looking for hippy paradise don't appeal to you for an overnight stay, you can make a day trip out of it by catching a boat from Bophut Beach (just south of the Oasis bungalows) on Koh Samui to Haad Rin on Koh Phangan. It leaves at 9:30 a.m., arrives an hour-and-a-half later at Chalok Lum, and makes the return trip at 2:30 p.m. The fare is 60 baht ($2.40). Excursions including lunch, for a minimum of four people, are sometimes available for 120 baht ($4.80).

If it's even more isolation you seek, you can continue

on past Koh Phangan to Koh Tao, a tiny island with breathtakingly clear and sheltered waters for swimming and snorkeling. You can actually swim with friendly sharks in the peaceful bay at Haad Nang Yuan. Bungalows are available on the western and southern beaches. The boat that leaves Bophut at 9:30 a.m. arrives at Mae Haad, Koh Tao, at 1:30 p.m.

Note: If you are traveling between May and October, when the weather can be unpredictable and schedules are apt to be disrupted, check with a Songserm office before making plans to travel by sea. In Bangkok, call (02) 250-0768, 252-5190, or 252-9654. On Koh Samui, call (077) 421-228, 421-078, or 421-316.

KOH PHANGAN TO KRABI

You spend this morning sailing the open sea in the Gulf
of Thailand, cruising past strangely shaped islands and
dramatic limestone formations, before transferring to the
air-conditioned bus that carries you across the narrow
isthmus of southern Thailand to the provincial capital of
Krabi. Before sunset, you are picking up shells along the
spectacular Ao Phra Nang.

Suggested Schedule

5:00 a.m.	Rise early for breakfast and ride to Thong Sala.
6:15 a.m.	Express boat to Koh Samui.
7:30 a.m.	Express boat from Koh Samui to Surat Thani.
10:00 a.m.	Air-conditioned bus to Krabi.
1:30 p.m.	Lunch and stroll through Krabi town.
3:30 p.m.	Songthaew or minibus to Phra Nang Beach.
4:00 p.m.	Check in at resort or bungalow. Explore the beach.
6:30 p.m.	Dinner. Evening at leisure.

Travel Route

The Songserm express boat leaves Thong Sala pier, Koh
Phangan, at 6:15 a.m., with one stop at Na Thon, Koh
Samui, then continuing to Ban Don pier with shuttle ser-
vice to Surat Thani. The entire trip takes about 3¼ hours.
The fare from Koh Phangan is 175 baht ($7). Songserm
coordinates all its schedules to mesh, and your bus to
Krabi leaves at 10:00 a.m. The 2½-hour bus ride across
the peninsula costs 300 baht ($12). A combined boat-
and-bus ticket is available from Koh Phangan or Koh
Samui.

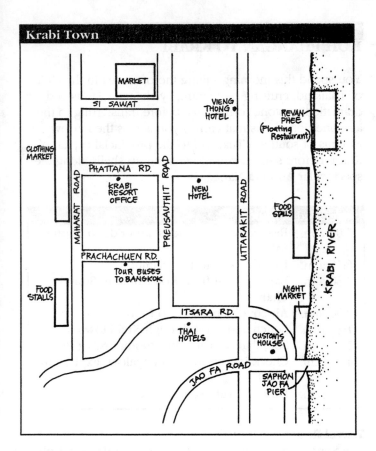

Krabi Town

Krabi

Southern Thailand is the narrow strip of land that
extends down from the Bangkok region, between the
Andaman Sea and the Gulf of Thailand to the border
with Malaysia. In many ways it is a world apart from the
north, with different geography, climate, natural vegetation, agriculture, history, and mix of religions. From the
eleventh into the thirteenth century, the independent
city-states of the peninsula were consolidated under the
Sivichaya Empire, governed from the distant island of

Sumatra. The empire disintegrated in the thirteenth century, and in 1350, the southern provinces, with a regional authority centered at Nakhon Si Thammarat, were brought into the kingdom of Ayutthaya. Although the governor of Nakhon Si Thammarat declared himself king of the area when Ayutthaya fell in 1767, the strategically important peninsular region was soon brought under the control of King Taksin. A century later, King Chulalongkorn, Rama V, tightened administrative control over the south by establishing provincial authorities under the leadership of Bangkok.

The modern transportation system and increased attention from the national government have created new ties that bind the south to the rest of Thailand, but the region still has significant distinguishing characteristics. Rubber production, coconut plantations, and tin mining are the mainstays of the prosperous southern economy. The influence of Islam is much more pronounced in the south. The local dialects and the regional cuisine are strongly influenced by the proximity to Malaysia.

Of the 14 provinces of southern Thailand, Krabi, located on the eastern shore of Phang Nga Bay, 40 km east of Phuket, may be the most beautiful. It is nicknamed the "Emerald of the Andaman Sea," and as clichéd as that sounds, the title is deserved. The landscape is a fantasia of eerie limestone cliffs jutting suddenly from the dense green jungle. Every side road seems to lead into the vine-laden entrances of mysterious caves. Limestone formations bolt out of the calm sea and assume haunting, shadowy shapes against a red dawn or a purple dusk. Krabi Province encompasses a pair of the world's most spectacular islands, Koh Phi Phi, plus splendid parks and gardens, and glorious white sand beaches. Tourism is a relatively recent phenomenon but is growing rapidly, and it may not be long before Krabi becomes the next Phuket, which only a few years ago was considered an unspoiled paradise.

Lodging
Krabi town is a wonderful place to explore and has several choices for accommodations, including the old **Thai Hotel** at 7 Issara Road, with 108 rooms at 140 to 400 baht ($5.60-$16), the **New Hotel** at 9-11 Pattana Road, with a dozen rooms priced from 100 to 120 baht ($4-$4.80), and the newest **Wiang Thong** at 155 U-Trakit Road, with 154 rooms from 140 to 800 ($5.60-$32).

The most pleasant base for a short visit to the province, however, has long been Ao Phra Nang, a gorgeous bay with a long stretch of beach situated about 25 minutes north of town. But it is building up rapidly. The **Krabi Resort** is an imposing operation, with 40 motel-style rooms overlooking a swimming pool and 45 fairly luxurious bungalows in a garden setting of palms, pine trees, and rolling lawns. The best choice here (despite the TV, minibar, etc.) is an air-conditioned beach-front bungalow. Prices range from 1,100 to 1,900 baht ($44-$76). An attractive open-air restaurant and bar overlooks the beach. Scuba diving, snorkeling trips, and day tours can all be arranged as well. Tel. (075) 612-161.

Phra-Nang Inn, just a few hundred meters down the beach, is a more modest alternative, with a variety of bungalows, twin and double rooms in a Thai-style motel setting for 900 to 1,100 baht ($36-$44). The rooms are clean and neatly appointed without straining for elegance, the restaurant serves delicious seafood and Thai dishes right over the waves, and the manager, Anuwat (Dominic) Thongsuk, is an especially gentle and solicitous host. Tel. (075) 612-173.

Ao Nang Villa competes with the Krabi Resort for the upscale market, offering bungalows from 750 baht ($30) and luxury rooms with hot tubs, mini bars, TV, etc. at rates of 1,400 baht ($56) to 2,200 baht ($88). Tel (075) 612-994.

A recently discovered retreat, **Dawn of Happiness Beach Resort**, is located on Ao Nam Mao Beach, about half-way between Krabi City and Ao Phra Nang. An eco-sensitive resort, operated by a Canadian ecologist, Dawn of Happiness offers beautifully appointed Thai-style bungalows in a beach/garden setting, with a genuine family ambience, ample opportunities to engage with the local population in day to day activities (fishing, rubber making, rice cultivation), and attention to recycling, organic agriculture, and environmental preservation (including the resort's own Youth Conservation Corps). Tel. (750) 612-730 (731), ext. 207.

Good low-end cottages and bungalows are available at **P. S. Cottages** for 120 to 200 baht ($4.80-$8), at **Peace Bungalow** for 50 to 200 baht ($2-$8), and up the hill at **Princess Garden** for 50 to 120 baht ($2-$4.80).

Food

The pride of Krabi Province is its seafood, and almost anywhere you go you can find fresh bonita, catfish, shark, prawns, crab, and lobster. **Ao Phra Nang** offers the delightful opportunity to "shop" for dinner. You can walk from bungalow to bungalow along the beach and check out the different displays of today's catch and compare prices. The seafood is generally sold by the kilogram — from 75 to 200 baht ($3-$8) per kilo. It's cooked to order on the barbecue and brought sizzling to your table. The **Krabi Beach Resort** also features an enormous menu of Thai and Western dishes averaging about 60 baht ($2.40) each, with the spices slightly toned down for sensitive palates. **Phra-Nang Inn** is again more modest but more authentic. The pad thai is especially good. You can get barbecued corn, potato, or chicken as well, and the fish is served with a tasty hot and spicy chutney. If you're in Krabi town at night, avoid the splashy floating restaurant that caters to tourists and try the fish, prawns, or crab balls at the **Kotung** restaurant near the pier. Or snack endlessly in the **night market**.

Sightseeing Highlights

▲▲**Ban Don**—The pier where the Songserm express boat arrives is more colorful than the town of Surat Thani itself. If you have a few minutes to walk around before making your bus connection, check out the great fruit market and the interesting market stalls around the waterfront. Note that sometimes weather conditions or port situations detour the express boats south to the dock at Donsak. If you land at Donsak, the slow sail into the bay is fascinating because of the large number of fishing families living right on the waterway. The fish processing plants are both an eyeful and a noseful. When such detours are necessary, Songserm buses meet passengers here for the hour ride to Surat Thani.

▲**Surat Thani**—Unlike most of the Thai cities and towns you've visited on this itinerary, Surat Thani actually has little to offer in the way of historical sights or cultural affairs. The town has built up over the years as a commercial hub, dealing in the trade and transportation of such essential southern products as rubber and coconut. It has a certain appeal as an average workaday city doing business with few distractions other than the tourists passing through. If you stop over for more than a few minutes and want a substantial snack, try the regional specialty, *khao kai op*, marinated baked chicken served with rice, at one of the food stalls in the Kaset Market next to the bus station.

▲▲▲**Krabi Town**—Because its links to the rest of Thailand have been confined to land and sea transport (the airport has long been rumored to be "about to open"), Krabi town still has the intriguing atmosphere of a provincial crossroads. Although the tourist bustle is picking up, evidenced by the growing number of tour entrepreneurs, the town is quiet compared with a more traveled city like Chiang Mai. The air is charged, however, by the unique mix of ethnic groups, the coexistence of Muslims and Buddhists, and the movement of international travelers heading north from Malaysia or south toward Hat Yai. You can almost feel the town's history as an outpost for smuggling whiskey and cigarettes. Krabi town is laid out north to south along the Krabi River. It is only about five blocks long and two to three blocks deep, so you can easily explore it by foot in an hour or two, peeking into the many bakeries, cafés, and markets. At night, young travelers tend to gather in the few bars and restaurants, and a night market is set up where the road curves west just north of the pier.

DAY 18
KRABI: A NATURAL WONDER

The topography and geology of Krabi Province are among Thailand's most amazing natural wonders. Today, you devote the morning to a land tour of caves, parks, and gardens. In the afternoon, choose among the variety of water sports available, from cruising between islands to scuba diving or just relaxing on the beach.

Suggested Schedule	
7:00 a.m.	Breakfast.
8:00 a.m.	Half-day tour of Krabi Province.
1:30 p.m.	Lunch.
2:30 p.m.	Swimming, sunning, snorkeling, or off-shore island tour.
6:30 p.m.	Barbecued seafood dinner. Evening at leisure.

Getting Around
In town, **Chan Phen Tour** and **Jungle Book**, on the main road along the water, offer full-day city and countryside tours that take in the Shell Cemetery, Tiger Cave Temple, Ao Luk Grotto, Than Bokkharani National Park and Botanical Gardens, and other sights for about 260 baht ($12.40) per person. Half-day excursions are available as well. Both the **Krabi Beach Resort** and **Phra-Nang Inn** have daily tour packages available for land exploration, boating excursions, and scuba diving. They range from 300 baht ($12) up to 2,000 baht ($80).

Sightseeing Highlights
▲▲▲**Susan Hoi Shell Cemetery**—About 5 km east of Ao Phra Nang and 7 km south from the main road that runs west out of Krabi town, the ancient sea floor has worked its way onto the beach. Large flat formations

angle up like ramps piled atop one another. But what from a distance look like concrete slabs are actually big rocklike sections of compressed, petrified seashells, estimated to be up to 75 million years old. On average, the slabs are layered with 50 centimeters of coal sandwiched between two 50-centimeter layers of fossilized shell. You can go hunting for shells at low tide or browse the selection of fossils and shell jewelry in the huts set up along the beach.

▲▲▲**Than Bokkharani National Park and Botanical Gardens**—Situated on Highway 4, the road north toward Ao Luk, this national park is one of the finest in Thailand. The setting of majestic cliffs, sparkling streams, cascading waterfalls, and meticulously maintained gardens is a Southeast Asian Shangri-la. Scores of paths wind through the lush foliage of the Botanical Gardens, leading to subterranean caverns, lagoons, and other tranquil spots.

▲▲**Ao Luk**—This subdistrict of Krabi Province, about 57 km north of Krabi town, is famous for the towering limestone monoliths that rise up out of the jungles and Ao Luk Bay. The jungle vegetation grows up and over the ridges of these prehistoric formations. Tours here usually stop at Tham Sra Yuan Tong, a grotto with a freshwater spring and pool. At the bay, boat rides are available to examine the fantastic Tham Lod, Tham Phi Hua To, and Tham Pra Tuu Saksit (the Godly Door), three caves (*tham*) in the great limestone walls. The first is full of stalactites and stalagmites, the second contains ancient paintings, and the third is notable for the rainbow colors of its limestone.

▲▲▲**Wat Tham Sua**—While central and northern Thailand have hundreds of major temples, the famous wats of southern Thailand are much fewer in number. This one, about 3 km northwest of Krabi town, is one of the most celebrated. Also known as the Tiger Cave Monastery, this forest wat is home to a community of about 250 Buddhist monks and nuns. Its most unique

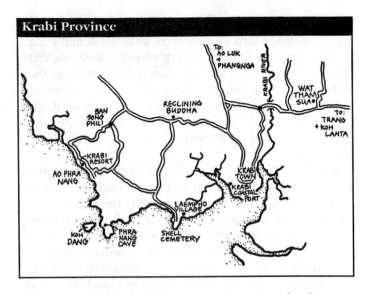

Krabi Province

features are the limestone caves and grottoes that have
been converted into monastic cells. The gruesome photographs of cadavers hung on some of the walls allegedly
stem from dissections the monks once conducted to gain
insight into the evil that possessed the living bodies. The
cave from which the monastery gets its name is up a
steep staircase to the left of the main chapel. Limestone
outcroppings create an image resembling a tiger's claw.
The Bow Cave and Eel Cave are nearby.

▲▲**Poda Islands**—Some fifteen picturesque islands are
located in Phra Nang Bay, including Chicken Island,
Turtle Island, and Poda Island. These have sandy beaches and the best coral reefs in the area. You can reach
them by a 30-minute long-tail boat ride from Phra Nang
at a cost of 250 to 700 baht ($10-$28) per person.
Snorkeling is fantastic here, and scuba dives can be
arranged as well.

ITINERARY OPTION: PHANG NGA

One of the most popular excursions in southern Thailand is a day trip to the geographically spectacular region of Phang Nga Bay, situated midway along the coastline between Krabi and Phuket. The entire province is studded with unusual limestone formations, beautiful waterfalls, and fascinating caves. But the main attraction, drawing a regular fleet of tour boats from Phuket, is the bay itself, made famous when it was used as the setting for the James Bond thriller, *The Man with the Golden Gun*. Buses run regularly along the Route 4 highway from Krabi to Phuket, with stops at Phang Nga. The 88-km trip takes about 90 minutes and costs 20 baht ($0.80). It is also possible to make the trip on motorbike. In Phang Nga, long-tail boats can be hired at the pier, Tha Don, for a water tour among the more than 100 islands of the bay. The four-hour boat ride costs about 500 baht ($20).

Sightseeing Highlights
▲▲**Suwan Khuha Cave**—Seven km outside the town of Phang Nga, on the way to the small village of Takua Thung, there is a turnoff to the right leading to this unusual cave, which has been incorporated into the temple known as Wat Suwan Khuha or Wat Tham. The cave is filled with Buddha images, chedis, and prangs tucked amongst the limestone stalactites and stalagmites.
▲▲▲**Tham Lod**—The water tour of Phang Nga Bay takes you through this amazing limestone cavern, a wide tunnel through one of the islands. If your guide shuts down his motor and lets the boat drift through the still waters, the only sounds you can hear are the eerily echoing drips of water from the dangling limestone prongs.
▲▲▲**Koh Pannyi**—Settled two centuries ago by Muslim immigrants from Malaysia, this "flag island" is now home to 1,200 villagers living in a fishing village built on stilts at the base of the towering island. The town mosque clings to the face of the great limestone cliff. Many tours

stop here for lunch. Some visitors stay overnight, hosted by an enterprising local guide named Sayan, who leads tours that start in the morning.

▲▲▲**Koh Phing Kan**—Popularly known as James Bond Island ever since 007 made his stop here, this highly photographed formation's name means "two islands leaning back to back." It took its present shape thousands of years ago when an earthquake shifted the footing and split the island vertically, with the two halves falling against each other at their peaks.

▲▲**Koh Tapu**—Another geological oddity, this limestone formation rises straight up out of the water to a height of 200 meters and is nicknamed "Nail Island" for its peculiar shape.

KRABI TO KOH PHI PHI

Today, you take a refreshing morning cruise across the Andaman Sea from Krabi to a spot that gives new meaning to the term "island paradise." The beauty of this matched pair of islands known as Koh Phi Phi surpasses anything captured on postcards. While the theme here is rest and relaxation, you also have the chance to get to the source of Bird's Nest Soup.

Suggested Schedule

7:00 a.m.	Breakfast at bungalow or resort. Check out.
8:00 a.m.	Drive into Krabi town for 9:30 a.m. express boat to Koh Phi Phi.
12:00 noon	Arrive at Koh Phi Phi. Check into bungalow. Lunch.
1:00 p.m.	Excursion to Phi Phi Le.
3:30 p.m.	Relax on beach.
6:00 p.m.	Dinner. Evening at leisure.

Travel Route

The express boat to Koh Phi Phi leaves every morning at 9:30 a.m. You can book your passage in advance at your resort or one of the travel services in Krabi town. The trip costs 150 baht ($6) and takes 2½ hours.

Koh Phi Phi

There may be no better or prettier place in Thailand to wind down completely than these twin enchanted islands. As you approach them from the east, their shapes mysteriously loom up out of the calm sea, appearing more and more magnificent as you come closer. Flying fish and dolphins sometimes swim alongside the boat, accompanying you toward paradise. The island

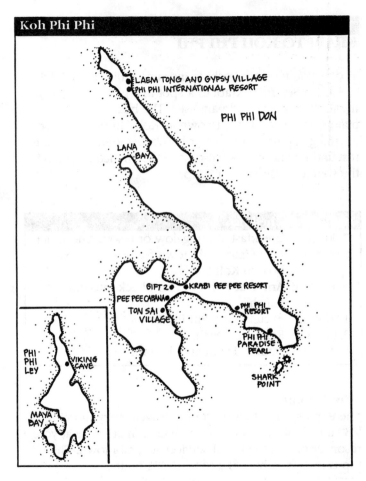

Koh Phi Phi

to the left (south), with the sheer northern cliff that seems to drop forever, is Phi Phi Le. It is uninhabited and accessible only for short visits to the giant cave where swallows' nests are collected by local gatherers. To the right (north) is Phi Phi Don, the larger of the pair and the location of the various Phi Phi bungalows and resorts. As you cruise slowly into Ton Sai Bay, the view of Phi Phi Don is spectacular. Giant limestone walls, overgrown with vegetation, climb to lofty heights on the left. Ahead is a stunning crescent of white sand, glowing beyond the multiple-shaded turquoise waters. The island has a unique double-crescent shape at this point, and just across a narrow strip of land from Ton Sai Bay is Lo Da Ram, another gorgeous bay enclosed by limestone cliffs.

Given its incomparable beauty, Koh Phi Phi is remarkable as one of the final holdouts from rampant tourism in the south. Hundreds of tourists from Phuket do take a day trip here, stopping at Ton Sai Bay for snorkeling and refreshments, cruising over to Phi Phi Le for a peek at the cave, and sailing around Phi Phi Don for a buffet lunch at the P. P. International Resort on the northern cape. But few stay for more than an hour or two. The travelers who do fill up the bungalows at Ton Sai Beach are seeking nothing more than tranquility and natural splendor, and that's just what they find. Chances are good, however, that in the coming years more development will take place and some of the budget cottages will be replaced by upscale resorts. But for now, even when it's crowded with farangs in the high season, Koh Phi Phi cannot be eclipsed for sheer beauty, peace, and quiet.

Lodging
Luxury amenities are available on Phi Phi Don at the **P. P. International Resort**, located at Cape Laemthong on the northeastern tip of the island. It overlooks a beautiful bay, good for swimming and snorkeling, and offers everything from scuba, fishing, hiking, and camping to deluxe air-conditioned rooms with television, telephone, refrigerator, and private balcony. Rates start at 1,500 baht ($60) for a single and go up to 2,100 baht ($84) for a deluxe double, plus an additional 250 baht ($10) high season room charge, 10 percent service charge, and 11 percent government tax. Reservations can be made through Bangkok at 121/7 Soi Chalermla, Phayathai Road, Bangkok 10400, tel. (02) 250-0768.

Located right in the middle of Ton Sai Beach, the **Pee Pee Island Cabana** operates over 100 bungalows nestled amongst the palms and right along the beach. Accommodations range from fairly spartan—small rooms, funky fans, old tile floors, cold water showers, no towels or view—to new, tidy cottages with porches along a garden path at the edge of the bay. The best bungalows are in the **Ton Sai Village** section, run by the same people, farther to the left (west) toward the cliff. Cabana rates are 500 baht ($20) for a fan twin, 1,100 ($44) for air-conditioned, plus service and tax. Ton Sai rates are 750 baht ($30) for a fan twin and 1,110 baht ($44) for air-conditioned.

Behind the Cabana, on the other bay, or to the right, toward the eastern curve of the bay, many more bungalows are available. Some are extremely spartan—mostly suitable for backpackers—but they are the best bargains. The **Gift 2 Bungalows**, the **Phi Phi Resort**, and others rent their hideaways for about 50 to 80 baht ($2-$3.20). Farther around the bay are the **Andaman**, with rooms for 50 to 180 baht ($2-$7.20), and the **Phi Phi Paradise Pearl**, with rates at 100 to 250 baht ($4-$10).

Food

If room rates on Phi Phi seem a little steep for what you get compared with the rest of Thailand, eating is still a bargain. Like Krabi, fish fresh off the boat is the staple. All along the walkway leading east from the Cabana around the bay, small restaurants with names like **Star, Phai, Phi Phi Bakery House & Pink Rose Restaurant, Kangaroo Restaurant**, and **Maikum Seafood** display their catch. Bonita, catfish, shark, lobsters, prawns, crabs, and other delicacies are laid out on ice for your viewing pleasure. A cook is tending a big oil-drum barbecue and grilling items on order. The prices can even be a little better here than at Krabi, starting at about 50 baht ($2) per kilo. You can also get good noodle, soup, and rice dishes along this strip for 30 to 75 baht ($1.20-$3). It's worth the walk out to the **Phi Phi Resort** at sunset to sit and snack at one of the bamboo tables on the rocky promontory overlooking the entire bay as the colors change in the sky and water.

Both the **Pee Pee Island Cabana** and **Ton Sai Village** have their own restaurants, offering fish, soups, rice, Thai curries, and Western foods at reasonable prices, about 50 to 75 baht ($2-$3) per dish. Breakfasts are 50 to 80 baht ($2-$3.20).

Sightseeing Highlights

▲▲▲**Viking Cave**—Phi Phi Don's uninhabited twin island, Phi Phi Le, is a natural preserve, available only for short visits. Choose from any of the boat operators at Ton Sai Bay and sign up for a long-tail boat trip that will take you to the Viking Cave and for a cruise around Phi Phi Le to Maya Bay, back to Phi Phi Don by way of Shark Point. It should cost about 100 baht ($4) per person for a half day. The prime attraction on Phi Phi Le is the Viking Cave, which gets its name from supposedly ancient wall drawings of various seagoing vessels. The real fascination, however, are the flimsy frameworks of bamboo "ladders" that zigzag their way to the top of the 80-meter-high cave. Daring local gatherers shinny up these structures to collect the nests of the swallows that migrate here each year. Every January through April, the unwary birds return to Phi Phi Le from all over southern Thailand. They use their saliva to fashion little cup-shaped nests on the walls of the cave. After the nests dry and harden, the men climb up and swipe them away and sell them to traders, who in turn market them to Chinese restaurants all over Asia. When the nests are cooked in broth, they become soft and translucent, and this great (and expensive) delicacy is highly valued. The best nests are the clear ones from the first round of building. After those disappear, the birds return and try again. This time there may be a little mud and dirt mixed in, bringing down the quality. By the the third or fourth try, the nests are no longer marketable,

and the gatherers finally let the swallows lay their eggs
and carry on with their genetic calling.
▲▲▲**Maya Bay**—This beautiful sheltered cove is located
on the southwestern side of Phi Phi Le. Its crystalline
waters and protected coral formations are ideal for snorkeling. (If you do not have your own mask and fins, be
sure to test the fit and comfort of the rental equipment
before you set out.)

KOH PHI PHI

You have seen many of the natural wonders of the region at or above sea level, so spend most of your final full day in the south of Thailand enjoying the rare bounty of the ocean. The Andaman Sea is widely treasured as an uncommonly beautiful and unspoiled underwater paradise. Whether you snorkel, scuba dive, or try your luck at fishing—the rewards can be astounding.

Suggested Schedule

8:00 a.m.	Breakfast.
9:00 a.m.	Scuba, snorkeling, or fishing excursion.
1:00 p.m.	Lunch.
2:00 p.m.	More scuba, snorkeling, or island exploration.
6:00 p.m.	Dinner. Evening at leisure.

Sightseeing Highlights

▲▲▲**Coral Reefs of Koh Phi Phi**—A handful of international locations are renowned for their spectacularly clear waters and abundant aquatic life: the Red Sea; Cozumel, Mexico; Australia's Great Barrier Reef; Palau, Micronesia. Thailand's reputation for first-rate scuba diving has grown dramatically in recent years, and many mainland and Phuket dive operations advertise overnight packages to Koh Phi Phi, where the fantasic land formations of jagged limestone outcroppings and lofty cliffs are mirrored underwater by striking pinnacles and sheer walls. The sea life is incredibly abundant. In shallow waters, you can merely dunk your face underwater and spy a tremendous variety of colorful fish and coral formations. If you do not scuba dive, at least put on a mask, snorkel, and fins and paddle around on the surface, gazing down on the amazing underwater world. Swim down only three to five meters and you will immerse yourself in living menageries of angelfish, parrot fish, clown fish, rays, and hundreds of varieties of living soft and hard coral in every color of the rainbow. Dive trips from Ton Sai Bay focus on the protected coves, caverns, and reefs around Phi Phi Le. Excursions are priced at about 750 baht ($30) for one scuba dive, 1,000 baht ($40) for two dives. Prices include equipment rental, lunch food, snack fruit, fresh water, the boat, and a dive guide.

You can treat yourself to an hour or so of good snorkeling right in Ton Sai Bay, where the coral formations start at depths of about three to four meters and increase in density and complexity the farther you swim from shore. If you plan to swim out, take a buddy and watch carefully for boat traffic in and out from the pier. The closer you are to the west end of the bay, near the cliff, the better. Snorkeling is even more rewarding around Cape Laemthong, location of the P. P. International Resort, and you can hire a long-tail boat to take you there. Don't forget to use extra protection from the sun when you are on or in the water.

Note: While most dive operations offer quick resort courses in scuba, providing you with NAUI or PADI certification at the end, these are not necessarily the safest ways to learn. If you plan to dive on your vacation, consider enrolling in an intensive water safety and scuba skills course before you leave home. There is no substitute for intimate familiarity with the equipment and procedures of scuba diving. Such knowledge comes only with serious study, rigorous training, and extensive experience. Underwater emergencies may not be terribly common, but they can have terrible consequences for the unknowledgeable and inadequately trained diver. The potential hazards are too great for you to take anything for granted. Even if you are an experienced diver, be sure to thoroughly examine the credentials and the equipment of the dive operation. Many divers like to carry at least their own regulators when they vacation in the tropics. Do not dive if you have any reservations about the safety of your proposed excursion, and never go underwater on a scuba dive without a buddy.

Also, as hardy as it looks, the ocean environment is very fragile. Coral is a colony of living animals and can be killed by the slightest touch of a human hand, let alone the violent flap of a flipper. Some formations take hundreds of years to grow a meter or two, and it is a great tragedy when they are knocked off and irreparably damaged by a careless movement or, worse, poached by a collector. It's the diver's responsibility to be conscientious about protecting the life underwater. Enough problems are posed by development and pollution without being exacerbated by sporting enthusiasts.

▲▲**Deep-sea Fishing**—Although tourism has become a major livelihood on Koh Phi Phi, the traditional occupation is fishing. You have probably already sampled the results, but several boat operators will gladly give you a chance to try your own hand. The sea is generous here, and the locals know all the best places to virtually guarantee some sort of catch. At the Pee Pee Cabana or at the Ton Sai pier, you can hire a boat for 600 baht ($24) for a half day, 800 baht ($32 baht) all day. A deep-sea fishing rig with a reel rents for another 200 baht ($8) half day, 400 baht ($16) full day. Or think of Spencer Tracy in *The Old Man and the Sea* and do your fishing in the traditional fashion with a hand line over the side of the boat. With any luck, you will bring back more than enough fresh fish to throw on the grill for your dinner.

KOH PHI PHI TO BANGKOK

Make the most of your last few hours on magical Koh
Phi Phi with a morning stroll along the bay or to the hilltop view point. Or take a final swim in the warm, gentle
surf. The rest of your day is spent in transit, by boat to
the large, popular island of Phuket and by plane back to
the "City of Angels," where you treat yourself to another
memorable Thai dinner and plan the final day of your
trip.

Suggested Schedule

7:30 a.m.	Morning walk.
9:00 a.m.	Breakfast.
11:00 a.m.	Prepare for departure. Check out.
12:00 noon	Lunch.
12:30 p.m.	Walk to the dock for 1:00 p.m. boat to Phuket.
3:00 p.m.	Arrive at Phuket. Transfer to bus for Phuket Airport.
5:00 p.m.	Check in for 6:00 p.m. flight to Bangkok.
7:15 p.m.	Arrive in Bangkok. Taxi to hotel.
8:30 p.m.	Dinner.

Travel Route

The boat from Koh Phi Phi to Phuket departs from the
main pier at Ton Sai Bay at 1:00 p.m., cruising around
the east side of Phi Phi Don, past Cape Laemthong, then
northeast through 23 nautical miles of typically calm seas
to Makham Bay near Phuket town. The trip takes two
hours and costs 250 baht ($10). The express boat serves
coffee, juice, and snacks along the way. Minibuses are
available for hire at the Makham Bay pier. You can ride
into Phuket town and transfer to a Thai Airways minibus

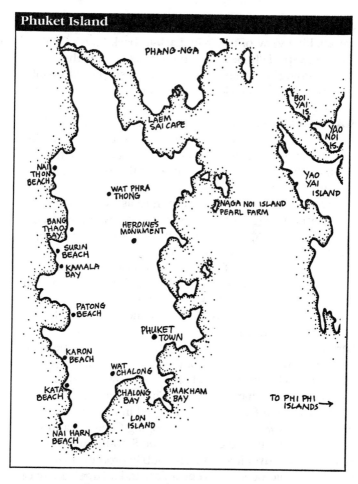

Phuket Island

or negotiate for a ride all the way to the airport. The 45-minute trip to the Phuket airport may cost 100 to 200 baht ($4-$8).

Sightseeing Highlights

▲▲**Phi Phi Don Hilltop View Point**—By walking east along Ton Sai Beach toward the southeastern tip of the island, you will find a trail that leads uphill between the Pee Pee Resort and the P. P. Andaman. The occasionally steep climb takes a half hour or so but is rewarded with a breathtaking view of the twin, back-to-back bays of Phi Phi Don, especially beautiful in the slanted sunlight of early morning. The view to Phi Phi Le is splendid as well, and on exceptionally clear days, you can see all the way to Phuket.

▲▲**Phuket Town**—Your ride from the boat dock to the airport might normally loop around Phuket town to avoid the dense traffic; many would consider that a blessing, given the heavy tourism orientation of this once-quaint provincial capital. But you probably have enough time before you need to be at the airport to ask your driver for a detour past some of the city's more interesting sights. Six km south of town is the island's most significant temple, Wat Chalong, an ornately bedecked building with a famous gilded statue of its revered turn-of-the-century abbot, Luang Pho Chaem. The town itself grew along with the development of tin production in Phuket Province. The most interesting architecture is concentrated in the northeast section, where the early twentieth-century tin barons built their mansions along the lines of European manors. Toward the center of town, several buildings retain the architectural blend of styles known as Sino-Portuguese: the Chartered Bank, Thai Airways, and the Provincial Town Hall, which was used in the filming of *The Killing Fields*. The Phuket Shopping Center is a modern, theme-parklike re-creation of the Sino-Portuguese style, full of souvenir shops. The public produce market sells fresh fruit, nuts, and vegetables, and a large variety of tropical flowers, especially Vanda orchids, are available from the nearby stalls. A drive up Rang Hill will give you the best view of the town and its environs. If you have time for a snack, stop at the Kanda Bakery at 31-33 Rasda Road for fresh baked goods and coffee or hot Thai curries and cold drinks. If a more leisurely lunch is feasible in your schedule, try the Kan Eang Restaurant south of town at the turnoff to Chalong Beach; all the drivers know where it is, because it has the best seafood on the island.

EXTRA DAY OPTION: PHUKET

Known as the "Pearl of the Andaman" and formerly called Koh Thalang, Phuket is Thailand's largest island, about the size of Singapore. It is separated from the mainland to the north by a narrow strip of water traversed by the Sarasin Bridge. Until recent years, it was the tropical paradise of southern Thailand. But tourism developed wildly in the 1970s and 1980s. The airport accepts large jetliners, and Phuket is now a featured destination on many group tour packages. The major beaches, once the unsullied pride of the island, have all been built up with resort hotels, bungalows, shopping arcades, discos, and bars. The indigenous culture has largely been swept out of sight, and tourist accommodations are geared not for the adventurer but for the pleasure seeker.

Yet, as much as it is threatening to develop into a new "Thai Riviera," Phuket is not without its redeeming values: its topography, water sports, and seafood. Once you've seen the island's beaches, you can understand the intense tourist migration and the corresponding building boom. Patong, on the western coast, is a gorgeous expanse of white sand with breathtaking views of the sunset. Consequently, it has been overrun with hotels, restaurants, discos, bars, bungalows, and beachside hawkers of everything from jewelry to massages. The other beaches have been subjected to varying degrees of the same "progress." The best for sunning or swimming extend from the northern end of the west coast to the southern tip. Nai Yang is pleasantly situated in a national park. Surin is home to the large PanSea Hotel and a nearby nine-hole golf course. Bang Tao has the big Dusit Laguna Hotel. Karon is the site of the enormous Le Meridian Phuket and Phuket Arcadia. Kata has the Club Med and so on through Nai Harn and around the cape to Rawai, Chalong, and Laem Phanwa.

Unlike Krabi and Koh Phi Phi, the Phuket resorts offer almost every kind of water recreation imaginable, from

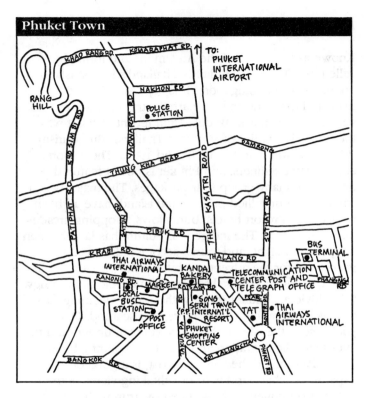

Phuket Town

snorkeling and scuba diving to surfing, windsurfing, sail-
boarding, waterskiing, jet skiing, and marlin fishing. The
greatest attractions for underwater enthusiasts lie fifty-six
nautical miles to the northwest. The Similan Islands are
one and a half to three hours away by boat and reward
the intrepid diver with scenes that eclipse those in most
other dive locations around the world. Because of their
remoteness, the nine Similans are almost virgin territory.
The walls and pinnacles are alive with sea fans, soft coral
trees, sponges, and anemones. The varieties of large,
open-water fish and exotic, brightly colored reef fish are
staggering. Phuket is worth a visit if only to arrange one
more day of diving in this phenomenal aquatic wilder-
ness. A one-day package with two dives, snacks, and

three meals (including barbecue dinner cruising back at sunset) may cost up to 3,000 baht ($120) through **Phuket Aquatic Safaris**, 62/9 Rasada Center, Rasada Road, Phuket 83000, tel. (076) 216-562. Overnight trips, with accommodations in park tents or longhouse rooms, are possible as well.

The newest additions to water recreation and sightseeing around southwestern Thailand are the expeditions offered by the **Phuket Sea Canoe Center**. They offer the most tranquil (and at the same time, the most stimulating) way to explore the Phang Nga caves and hongs, as you glide along the glassy water and slip through arches and other limestone formations that cannot be negotiated by larger craft. Options include everything from day trips at about 2,500 baht ($100) per person, to overnight, three-day, and week-long excursions. (The latter circumnavigates the Gulf of Phuket.) These outings, which include meals and transfers, are drawing rave reviews from novices and more experienced adventurers. It's wise to reserve in advance through Box 276, Phuket, Thailand 83000, fax (076) 213-934.

Lodging

Despite Phuket's popularity, you can still find secluded hideaways around the island. One beach that offers the full range of options in a relatively unspoiled setting is Nai Harn, a beautiful crescent-shaped bay on the southern tip of the island's west coast. If you want to rough it in the approximate backpacker's style of Koh Phangan, **Sunset Bungalows** has 65 minimal cottages staggered along rocky paths on the eastern hillside. The wooden rooms are spartan but rent for only 100 baht ($4) per night and have a wonderful view of the bay and a virtually private corner of the beach. The small open-air restaurant serves simple, home-cooked breakfasts and Thai soups, noodles, and rice dishes. The **Jungle Beach Resort** is the midrange option here, with prices ranging from 500 to 1,800 baht ($20-$72). You sacrifice being right on the bay for neatly appointed, comfortable rooms in a secluded, woodsy setting.

If after three weeks of travel you are ready to treat yourself to a dose of tropical luxury, the **Phuket Yacht Club**, dominating the western hillside on Nai Harn, is the prime choice. Everything here is geared for the tourist who wants to be pampered in exclusive surroundings. The hotel has a swimming pool overlooking the bay, a choice of restaurants serving elaborate Thai, continental, and seafood spreads, and deluxe rooms with private balconies and spectacular views of the sunrise. Management has given every attention to detail, from welcoming fruit baskets to skylights in the bathrooms. With only 108 rooms terraced above the bay, the Yacht Club doesn't accept large tour groups, avoiding the crowded feeling of many of Phuket's large resorts and providing ample opportunity for privacy. Casual elegance is the rule of thumb. The service is graciously doting without being overbearing or haughty. If you feel you deserve a splurge, this is the place to do it. But you really pay for it: 4,700 baht ($188) for a single, 5,400 ($216) twin; one- and two-bedroom suites are available from 7,000 baht ($280); tel. (076) 381-156 or Bangkok office (02) 254-5335.

Sightseeing Highlights
▲▲**Heroines' Monument**—It is rare that you see statues in Thailand erected to legendary women in the country's history, so this monument is of interest at least from an oblique feminist angle. The sisters represented here by two life-size bronze statues are Khunying Chan and Khunying Muk, who led the defense of Phuket's fortress during the Burmese invasion of 1785. King Rama I recognized their heroic effort of leading the island's army into victorious battle by granting them noble status. The monument is located on Highway 402 about halfway between Phuket town and the airport.

▲▲**Wat Phra Thong**—The Temple of the Golden Buddha is another spot rich with Thai folklore. Legend has it that a boy tethered his water buffalo to a post here and sometime later both the boy and the animal fell mysteriously ill. Then the boy's father, following messages received in a dream, found a spot where a metal stick rose from the ground and unearthed the topknot of a solid gold Buddha image. They were able to unearth only half the statue, and ever since, those who have tried to complete the task have met with strange and unfortunate results. Burmese invaders in 1785 were attacked by hornets when they attempted to loot the figure. Villagers later built the present temple to protect the revered image. It is located 6 km north of the Heroines' Monument.

▲▲**Naga Noi Pearl Farm**—Located off the northeastern tip of Phuket, 25 km north of Phuket town, the small island of Naga Noi features Thailand's largest cultured pearl farm. Tours are organized from town, or you can travel independently and take a small boat for the 20-minute ride across the Po Bay. Pearls are said to be less expensive here than even in the pearl markets of Japan.

▲▲**Wat Chalong**—At the beginning of the twentieth century, a legendary monk named Luang Pho Chaem was the abbot of this wat. When the armies of China and Malaysia attempted to overrun Phuket town and seize the vital tin mines, the monk's unique talent for setting bones proved extremely valuable in caring for the injured defenders. The gilded temple, probably the only truly outstanding building of the island's countryside, is best known for its rich adornments of colored and mirrored glass and the goldleaf-covered statue of the famous abbot. The wat is 6 km south of town, off the road to Chalong.

Helpful Hint
The local T.A.T. office is at 73-75 Phuket Road, Amphoe Muang, Phuket 83000, tel. (076) 212-213.

BANGKOK: ONE MORE TIME

Today is your last chance to absorb a bit more of the wild and amazing world of Bangkok. Choose among sightseeing, shopping, or getting a closer glimpse of people's lives by cruising the city's smaller canals. Treat yourself to a bargain buffet lunch and a final dinner of exquisite Thai cuisine at your favorite or new choice of restaurant.

Suggested Schedule

6:00 a.m.	Early breakfast at hotel.
7:30 a.m.	Klong tour.
12:00 noon	Buffet lunch at the Siam-Intercontinental Hotel.
1:00 p.m.	Shopping, sightseeing.
7:00 p.m.	Dinner. Prepare for departure.

Lodging Option

Perhaps the prospect of another day in Bangkok (including a Mister Toad's wild taxi ride into town) is too daunting; you could return only for a convenient overnight stay at the Amari Airport Hotel to make your flight connection home. It's located at 333 Choet Wudhakat Road, directly across the highway from Don Muang International Airport. Although the rates are not inexpensive at 3,300 baht ($132) for a single and 3,500 baht ($140) for a double, the convenience might make the expense worthwhile. (A special "Executive Floor" is available at higher prices.) A long overpass connects the hotel to the International terminal (luggage carts are provided free of charge at either end), and shuttle service is available into central Bangkok if you just have to get in a little more shopping or one more meal. The rooms are almost luxurious, with mini-bars, refrigerators, televisions, and

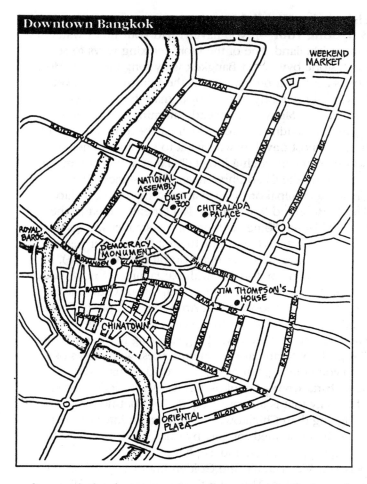

radios, and, thanks to soundproofing, are virtually free of the omnipresent jet roar of the airport. The hotel is riddled with restaurants, bars, lounges, and shops and offers many services, including sauna and massage. For daytime stopovers, a three-hour mini-stay for resting and freshening up is available from 8 a.m. to 6 p.m. at 450 baht ($18) for a twin room. Tel. 566-1020.

Sightseeing Highlights

▲▲Klong Tour—If you haven't had your fill of water trips in Thailand, one of the more relaxing ways to see the historic byways of Bangkok is by long-tail boat. Most hotels have tour desks, such as the Educational Travel Service in the lobby of the Royal, that offer package klong tours. Many include early morning rides to the Thonburi Floating Market, which has become a waste of time for most travelers who want to see any authentic action. You can catch a long-tail taxi at any of the major piers along the Chao Phrya River; for instance, Tha Chang near Silpakorn University and the Grand Palace, Tha Tien behind Wat Pho, or Tha Orienten next to the Oriental Hotel. Some set tours of the smaller klongs are available for anywhere from 10 baht ($0.40) per person up to 500 baht ($20) per boatload (about 10 people). If you've grown comfortable with bargaining by now, you can negotiate your own trip. Perhaps you would like to stop for a closer look at Wat Arun (the Temple of Dawn) on the Thonburi side of the river or cruise by the great shed that houses the royal barges. Klong Mon and Klong Bang Khow Wiang are common routes, with views of riverside housing, temples, and orchid farms.

▲▲Chinatown—Bangkok has its own Chinese section of the city that is less precisely defined but no less intriguing than Chinatowns in other great international cities. It is bounded roughly by Charoen Krung, Songsawat, Songwat, and Triphet roads, or the area between Wat Traimit (the Golden Buddha) and the Memorial Bridge. The main thoroughfare for a walking tour is Sampeng Lane (Soi Wanit 1), running east from the Pahurat Cloth Market to Wat Samphan Thainong. Along this famous lane you can find Chinese medicines, bird's nests, dyes, gold, cutlery, batiks, jewelry, hats, monk's supplies, hardware, woodcuts, rice paper, tools and hardware, and fabric and tailoring shops. More goods, produce, and food items are available along the parallel Yaowaraj Road and narrow Itsaranuphap Lane.

Nakhon Kasem, the Thieves' Market, is located in the northwest corner of Chinatown, framed by Charoen Krung, Yaowaraj, Boriphat, and Chakkrawat roads. Musical instruments, antiques, furniture, brass goods, and more are for sale here. Just the other side of Boriphat Road, along a north-south klong, is the Klong Ong Ang Market, specializing in all kinds of fish. Once you've started walking anywhere in the Chinatown area, you will want to explore every back alley and winding lane.

▲▲**Pahurat**—This cloth market at the northwestern edge of Chinatown, near a corner of Pahurat Road at the end of Soi Wanit, is also known as the Indian District. Many of the shop owners are Sikhs, specializing in the import of fabrics. People from all over the city come here to shop among the stalls for shoulder bags, unfinished yardage, and a variety of household goods that are less expensive here than in other Bangkok markets.

▲▲**Shopping**—Chinatown is only one of the many fascinating areas for shopping in Bangkok. If you are in that area, be sure to stroll through the Oriental Plaza—an upscale shopping arcade behind the Oriental Hotel—for stunning displays of antique sculptures, wood carvings, ivory, jewelry, cast images, and furnishings. The streets in the immediate vicinity of the Oriental and Shangri-La hotels, as well as the entire length of Silom Road northwest to Lumpini Park, are rife with stores selling designer-copy clothes, luggage, ivory, gems, leather work, gold and silver jewelry, and silk. Thai Home Industries, 35 Oriental Lane, for instance, is not only an outlet for crafts from all over Thailand (at surprisingly reasonable prices for Bangkok) but the originator of an internationally renowned flatware (with bowls and accessories) of hand-pounded bronze and stainless steel. The Jim Thompson Thai Silk Company, one of the most famous silk outlets in Bangkok, is at 9 Suriwongse Road, near the intersection with Rama IV Road. A ride to Rama I Road will take you to Siam Square (right next to the Siam Intercontinental Hotel), an immense shopping center organized around three major movie theaters: Scala, Lido, and Siam. Restaurants, book shops (including DK Books), cafés, electronics stores, and travel offices are abundant here. If you continue east, past where Rama I becomes Sukhumvit, you come upon block after block of stores selling books, stationery, clothing, folk art, and handicrafts. By riding north from the Democracy Monument on Paholyotin Road, you can reach Chatuchak Park, site of the enormous Weekend Market, Saturdays and Sundays from 9:00 a.m. to 6:00 p.m. This is like a giant flea market, with vendors selling used clothes, household items, army surplus goods, fabrics, leather goods, birds and bird cages, fish, flowers, and fresh produce.

▲▲**The National Assembly**—The modern capital area of Bangkok, near Wat Benchamabopit (the Marble Temple) at the intersection of Sri Ayutthaya and Rama V roads, includes this splendorous white marble building constructed in 1907 as King Chulalongkorn's Throne Hall. The square in front of the building, overseen by a statue of the beloved king on horseback, is a gathering place for important national celebrations, including the king's birthday. Spacious and beautiful Amporn Park lies right across the street. The annual Red Cross Fair is held here in January.

▲▲**Vimarn Mek**—Behind the National Assembly stands this "Cloud Mansion," reputedly the largest golden teak building in the world. The 100-room mansion was built as King Chulalongkorn's suburban family residence in 1900 and is brimming with crystal and European art objects.

▲**Chitralada Palace**—Located west of the National Assembly on Si Ayutthaya Road, the current residence of the king is not open to the public, so a partial view of its Thai-style buildings is all you get from the street. Construction on the vast grounds was initiated by Rama VI.

▲▲**Dusit Zoo**—If you want to see what many Bangkok families do for weekend outings, take a walk through this modern menagerie of monkeys, "white" elephants, hippos, kangaroos, bears, and birds. Formally called Khao Din ("Mountain of Earth"), the zoo is located between the Palace and the National Assembly and is open daily from 8:00 a.m. to 6:00 p.m.; admission is about 10 baht ($0.40).

▲▲**Jim Thompson's House**—After World War II, an American entrepreneur named Jim Thompson settled in Thailand and did much to boost international interest in Thai silk. One of Thompson's contributions was the introduction of colorfast dyes to replace the traditional vegetable dyes. For two decades, he built up his trade and invested the bulk of his earnings in collections of Asian art and antiques. Then, in 1967, while visiting the Cameron Highlands of the Malaysian Peninsula, Thompson mysteriously disappeared without a trace. His heirs decided to keep his mansion—a medley of seven traditional teak Thai-style houses— just as he left it. Even during his lifetime, Thompson's house was a virtual museum, drawing praise from W. Somerset Maugham for its design, decoration, and exhibits. Its construction, alongside a typical klong, is a model of traditional residential architecture. Inside, its teak-paneled rooms house huge collections of five-colored Bencharong porcelain (Chinese-made for export to Thailand), Ming pottery, Burmese wood carvings and statues, ancient Buddha images, rare doors, tables, collector's items that reflect Thompson's idiosyncratic tastes, and of course a great deal of Jim Thompson silk. The lush gardens surrounding the house are notable in their own right. The Jim Thompson House is on Soi Kasem San 2, Rama I Road, across from the National Stadium. It's open Monday through Saturday, 9:00 a.m. to 5:00 p.m., admission 125 baht ($5).

Departure

Remember to reconfirm your reservations for the flight
home at least 24 hours in advance. Check-in for international flights is two hours before scheduled departure.
Allow at least 45 minutes for your ride to Don Muang
International Airport, since the only thing predictable
about Bangkok traffic is its propensity for slowdowns
and impenetrable jams. The usual price for a taxi is 200
baht. At the airport, be ready for the worst possible sce-
narios: long lines for check-in, half-hour waits at immigration, long backups at security screenings. We've used
up our entire two hours in such delays. But we've also
breezed through in minutes. It all depends on how much
traffic and how many travelers the airport is handling that
day. Don't forget to save 200 baht ($8) per person for the
airport departure tax.

Other Books from John Muir Publications

Asia Through the Back Door, 4th ed., 400 pp. $16.95 (available 7/93)

Belize: A Natural Destination, 336 pp. $16.95

Costa Rica: A Natural Destination, 2nd ed., 310 pp. $16.95

Elderhostels: The Students' Choice, 2nd ed., 304 pp. $15.95

Environmental Vacations: Volunteer Projects to Save the Planet, 2nd ed., 248 pp. $16.95

Europe 101: History & Art for the Traveler, 4th ed., 350 pp. $15.95

Europe Through the Back Door, 11th ed., 432 pp. $17.95

Europe Through the Back Door Phrase Book: French, 160 pp. $4.95

Europe Through the Back Door Phrase Book: German, 160 pp. $4.95

Europe Through the Back Door Phrase Book: Italian, 168 pp. $4.95

Europe Through the Back Door Phrase Book: Spanish & Portuguese, 288 pp. $4.95

A Foreign Visitor's Guide to America, 224 pp. $12.95

Great Cities of Eastern Europe, 256 pp. $16.95

Guatemala: A Natural Destination, 336 pp. $16.95

Indian America: A Traveler's Companion, 4th ed., 448 pp. $17.95 (available 7/93)

Interior Furnishings Southwest, 256 pp. $19.95

Mona Winks: Self-Guided Tours of Europe's Top Museums, 2nd ed., 448 pp. $16.95

Opera! The Guide to Western Europe's Great Houses, 296 pp. $18.95

Paintbrushes and Pistols: How the Taos Artists Sold the West, 288 pp. $17.95

The People's Guide to Mexico, 9th ed., 608 pp. $18.95

Ranch Vacations: The Complete Guide to Guest and Resort, Fly-Fishing, and Cross-Country Skiing Ranches, 2nd ed., 396 pp. $18.95

The Shopper's Guide to Art and Crafts in the Hawaiian Islands, 272 pp. $13.95

The Shopper's Guide to Mexico, 224 pp. $9.95

Understanding Europeans, 272 pp. $14.95

Undiscovered Islands of the Caribbean, 3rd ed., 288 pp. $14.95

Undiscovered Islands of the Mediterranean, 2nd ed., 224 pp. $13.95

Undiscovered Islands of the U.S. and Canadian West Coast, 288 pp. $12.95

Unique Colorado, 112 pp. $10.95 (available 6/93)
Unique Florida, 112 pp. $10.95 (available 7/93)
Unique New Mexico, 112 pp. $10.95 (available 6/93)
A Viewer's Guide to Art: A Glossary of Gods, People, and Creatures, 144 pp. $10.95
The Visitor's Guide to the Birds of the Eastern National Parks: United States and Canada, 410 pp. $15.95

2 to 22 Days Series

Each title offers 22 flexible daily itineraries useful for planning vacations of any length. Aside from valuable general information, included are "must see" attractions *and* hidden "jewels."

2 to 22 Days in the American Southwest, 1993 ed., 176 pp. $10.95

2 to 22 Days in Asia, 1993 ed., 176 pp. $9.95

2 to 22 Days in Australia, 1993 ed., 192 pp. $9.95

2 to 22 Days in California, 1993 ed., 192 pp. $9.95

2 to 22 Days in Europe, 1993 ed., 288 pp. $13.95

2 to 22 Days in Florida, 1993 ed., 192 pp. $10.95

2 to 22 Days in France, 1993 ed., 192 pp. $10.95

2 to 22 Days in Germany, Austria, & Switzerland, 1993 ed., 224 pp. $10.95

2 to 22 Days in Great Britain, 1993 ed., 192 pp. $10.95

2 to 22 Days Around the Great Lakes, 1993 ed., 192 pp. $10.95

2 to 22 Days in Hawaii, 1993 ed., 192 pp. $9.95

2 to 22 Days in Italy, 208 pp. $10.95

2 to 22 Days in New England, 1993 ed., 192 pp. $10.95

2 to 22 Days in New Zealand, 1993 ed., 192 pp. $9.95

2 to 22 Days in Norway, Sweden, & Denmark, 1993 ed., 192 pp. $10.95

2 to 22 Days in the Pacific Northwest, 1993 ed., 192 pp. $10.95

2 to 22 Days in the Rockies, 1993 ed., 192 pp. $10.95

2 to 22 Days in Spain & Portugal, 192 pp. $10.95

2 to 22 Days in Texas, 1993 ed., 192 pp. $9.95

2 to 22 Days in Thailand, 1993 ed., 180 pp. $9.95

22 Days (or More) Around the World, 1993 ed., 264 pp. $12.95

Automotive Titles

How to Keep Your VW Alive, 15th ed., 464 pp. $21.95
How to Keep Your Subaru Alive 480 pp. $21.95
How to Keep Your Toyota Pickup Alive 392 pp. $21.95
How to Keep Your Datsun/Nissan Alive 544 pp. $21.95
The Greaseless Guide to Car Care Confidence, 224 pp. $14.95
Off-Road Emergency Repair & Survival, 160 pp. $9.95

TITLES FOR YOUNG READERS AGES 8 AND UP

"Kidding Around" Travel Guides for Young Readers
All the "Kidding Around" Travel guides are 64 pages and $9.95 paper, except for **Kidding Around Spain** and **Kidding Around the National Parks of the Southwest**, which are 108 pages and $12.95 paper.

Kidding Around Atlanta
Kidding Around Boston,2nd ed.
Kidding Around Chicago, 2nd ed.
Kidding Around the Hawaiian Islands
Kidding Around London
Kidding Around Los Angeles
Kidding Around the National Parks of the Southwest
Kidding Around New York City, 2nd ed.
Kidding Around Paris
Kidding Around Philadelphia
Kidding Around San Diego
Kidding Around San Francisco
Kidding Around Santa Fe
Kidding Around Seattle
Kidding Around Spain
Kidding Around Washington, D.C., 2nd ed.

"Extremely Weird" Series for Young Readers. Written by Sarah Lovett, each is 48 pages and $9.95 paper.
Extremely Weird Bats
Extremely Weird Birds
Extremely Weird Endangered Species
Extremely Weird Fishes
Extremely Weird Frogs
Extremely Weird Insects
Extremely Weird Mammals (available 8/93)
Extremely Weird Micro Monsters (available 8/93)
Extremely Weird Primates
Extremely Weird Reptiles
Extremely Weird Sea Creatures
Extremely Weird Snakes (available 8/93)
Extremely Weird Spiders

"Masters of Motion" Series for Young Readers. Each title is 48 pages and $9.95 paper.
How to Drive an Indy Race Car
How to Fly a 747
How to Fly the Space Shuttle

"X-ray Vision" Series for Young Readers. Each title is 48 pages and $9.95 paper.
Looking Inside Cartoon Animation
Looking Inside Sports Aerodynamics

Looking Inside the Brain
Looking Inside Sunken Treasure
Looking Inside Telescopes and the Night Sky

Multicultural Titles for Young Readers
Native Artists of North America, 48 pp. $14.95 hardcover
**The Indian Way: Learning to Communicate with Mother
Earth,** 114 pp. $9.95
The Kids' Environment Book: What's Awry and Why, 192 pp.
$13.95
Kids Explore America's African-American Heritage, 112 pp.
$8.95
Kids Explore America's Hispanic Heritage, 112 pp. $7.95

Environmental Titles for Young Readers
**Rads, Ergs, and Cheeseburgers: The Kids' Guide to Energy
and the Environment,** 108 pp. $12.95
Habitats: Where the Wild Things Live, 48 pp. $9.95
The Kids' Environment Book: What's Awry and Why, 192 pp.
$13.95

Ordering Information
Please check your local bookstore for our books, or call
1-800-888-7504 to order direct from us. All orders are shipped
via UPS; see chart below to calculate your shipping charge to
U.S. destinations. **No P.O. Boxes please; we must have a
street address to ensure delivery.** If the book you request is
not available, we will hold your check until we can ship it. Foreign orders will be shipped surface rate unless otherwise
requested; please enclose $3.00 for the first item and $1.00 for
each additional item.

For U.S. Orders Totaling	Add
Up to $15.00	$4.25
$15.01 to $45.00	$5.25
$45.01 to $75.00	$6.25
$75.01 or more	$7.25

Methods of Payment
Check, money order, American Express, MasterCard, or Visa.
We cannot be responsible for cash sent through the mail. For
credit card orders, include your card number, expiration date,
and your signature, or call (800) 888-7504. American Express
card orders can be shipped only to billing address of card-
holder. Sorry, no C.O.D.'s. Residents of sunny New Mexico, add
6.125% tax to total.

Address all orders and inquiries to:
    John Muir Publications
    P.O. Box 613
    Santa Fe, NM 87504
    (505) 982-4078
    (800) 888-7504